QUILT-LOVERS' FAVORITES™

FROM AMERICAN PATCHWORK & QUILTING®

Better Homes and Gardens® Creative Collection™
Des Moines, Iowa

VOLUME 5

Better Homes and Gardens®

QUILT-LOVERS' FAVORITES™

FROM AMERICAN PATCHWORK & QUILTING®

Printing Number and Year: 5 4 3 2 1 04 03 02 01

ISSN: 1532-8848 ISBN: 0-696-22121-7

For book editorial questions, write:
Better Homes and Gardens Quilt-Lovers' Favorites • *1716 Locust St., Des Moines, IA 50309-3023*

TREASURED QUILTS

Everything old became new again in Quilt-Lovers' Favorites™ *Volume 5, the newest book from* American Patchwork & Quilting® *magazine. We turned to pages of the magazine as the basis for this book because you, our readers, have told us that some of your all-time favorite designs exist there. We selected 15 classic designs, then pulled out fabric stashes and sketchbooks and created all-new projects based on those time-tested projects. From table runners to pillows to bed-size quilts to framed art—you're sure to find a project or two that meets your needs.*

So select a favorite project, follow our hallmark step-by-step instructions and full-size patterns, and use the color photographs and illustrations to create a gift for yourself or for someone else. A chart for optional sizes accompanies the main projects. Turn to the back of the book for Quilter's Schoolhouse, a section of useful information that will act as a foundation for building your quilting skills.

Heidi Kaisand

Executive Editor, American Patchwork & Quilting®

TABLE of CONTENTS

CLASSICS FOR TODAY

Page **6**

8 PINWHEEL SWIRL
12 Optional Sizes
12 Kid's Quilt
14 Wall Hanging

16 MANY TRIPS AROUND THE WORLD
19 Picnic Cloth
22 Baby Quilt

24 TURKEY TRACKS
28 Optional Sizes
29 Bed Quilt
31 Wall Hanging

BRIGHT AND COLORFUL

Page **34**

36 MISSISSIPPI WHEEL OF FORTUNE
43 Bed Quilt
46 Table Topper

48 SUNRISE, SUNSET
54 Wall Art
55 Throw

58 BALI HO
62 Floor Pillow
63 Throw

Page 66

68 FLICKERING STARS
73 Optional Sizes
74 Bed Quilt

76 DOLLY MADISON'S STAR
80 Optional Sizes
81 Scrappy Throw
83 Wall Hanging

86 SUNSHINE AND SHADE
90 Optional Sizes
90 Pillow
92 Wall Hanging

BITS AND PIECES

Page 94

96 CENTENNIAL PINEAPPLE
100 Optional Sizes
101 Pillow
102 Tree Skirt

104 JACOB'S LADDER
108 Tote Bag
110 Table Topper

112 RULE THE ROOST
117 Framed Art
118 Table Runner

ELEGANT APPLIQUÉ

Page 120

122 POINSETTIA
126 Optional Sizes
126 Tablecloth
128 Throw

130 TWELVE TRUMPETS
135 Wool Penny Rug
138 Bed Quilt

140 SWEET CHERRIES
146 Curtains
147 Bed Quilt

150 QUILTER'S SCHOOLHOUSE
150 Getting Started
151 Rotary Cutting
153 Cutting with Templates
154 Piecing
156 Appliqué
157 Cutting Bias Strips
158 Covered Cording
158 Hanging Sleeves
159 Finishing

160 CREDITS

CLASSICS FOR TODAY

For centuries, quilters have carefully sewn pieces that warm body and soul. Their craftsmanship and graphic design inspire admiration. Let the striking "Pinwheel Swirl," the intricate "Many Trips Around the World," and the charming "Antique Turkey Tracks" encourage you to stitch your own keepsake for future generations to treasure.

PINWHEEL *Swirl*

Editor Heidi Kaisand considers this antique quilt one of the jewels in her personal collection. Although the quiltmaker is unknown, Heidi's family remembers it always being a part of her great-grandmother's home.

Materials

4¼ yards of muslin for blocks, sashing, and border

5⅜ yards of solid red for blocks, sashing, and binding

4⅞ yards of backing fabric

73×87" of quilt batting

Finished quilt top: 67×81"
Finished block: 4" square

Quantities specified for 44/45"-wide, 100% cotton fabrics. All measurements include a ¼" seam allowance. Sew with right sides together unless otherwise stated.

Cut the Fabrics

To make the best use of your fabrics, cut the pieces in the order that follows.

From muslin, cut:

- 8—2×42" strips for border
- 143—3⅜" squares
- 546—2½" squares

From solid red, cut:

- 8—2½×42" binding strips
- 273—2½×4½" rectangles
- 286—2⅞" squares, cutting each in half diagonally for a total of 572 triangles
- 130—2½" squares

Assemble the Blocks

1. Sew a pair of solid red triangles to opposite edges of a muslin 3⅜" square (see Diagram 1). Press the seam allowances toward the solid red triangles.

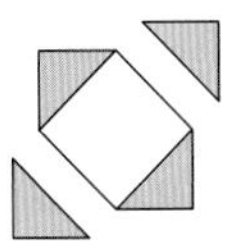

Diagram 1

continued

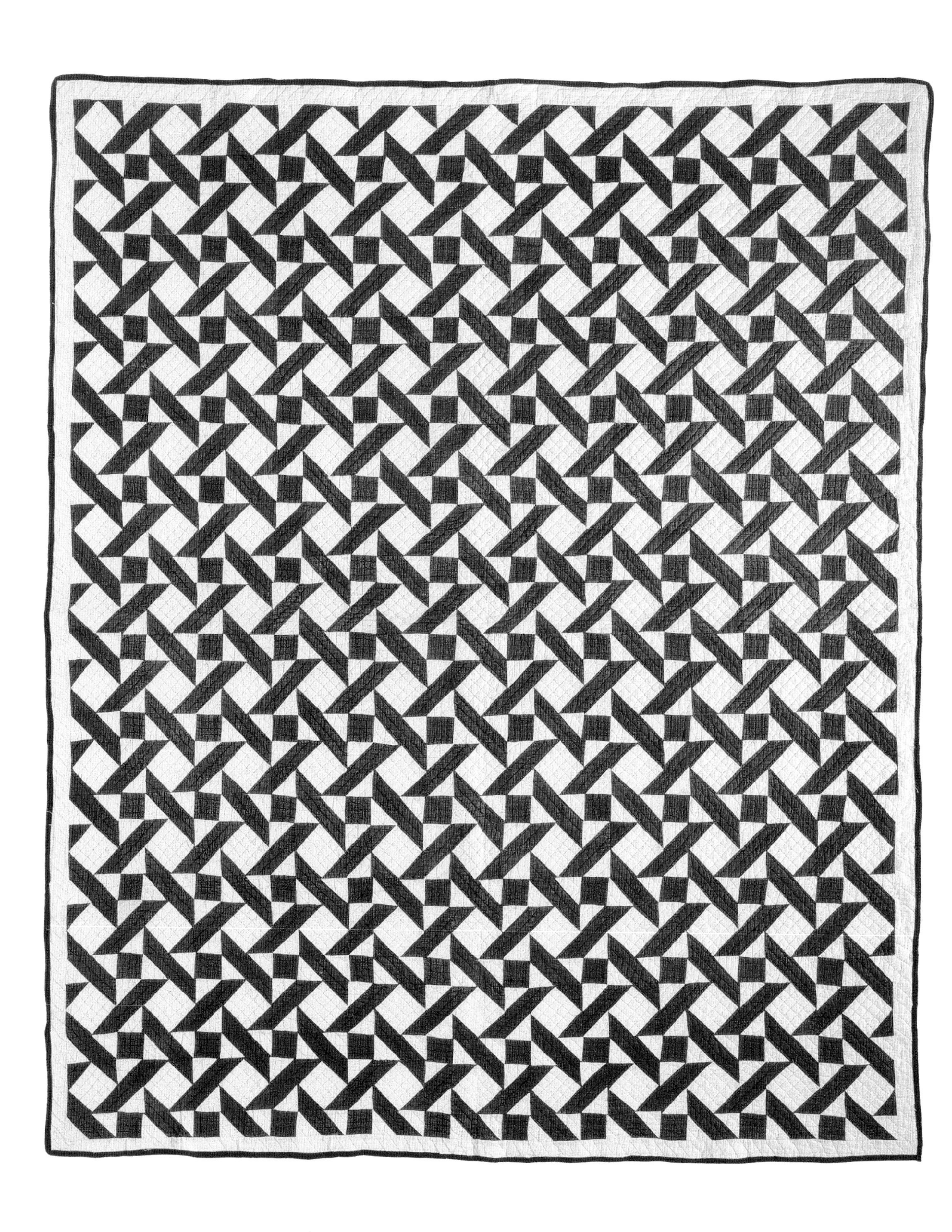

2. Add solid red triangles to the muslin square's remaining raw edges to make a square-in-a-square block. The pieced block should measure 4½" square, including the seam allowances.

3. Repeat steps 1 and 2 to make a total of 143 square-in-a-square blocks.

Assemble the Sashing Units

1. For accurate sewing lines, use a quilter's pencil to mark a diagonal line on the wrong side of each muslin 2½" square. (To prevent your fabric from stretching as you draw the lines, place 220-grit sandpaper under the squares.)

2. Align a marked muslin 2½" square with one end of a solid red 2½×4½" rectangle (see Diagram 2; note the placement of the marked diagonal line). Stitch on the marked line; trim the seam allowance to ¼". Press the attached triangle open.

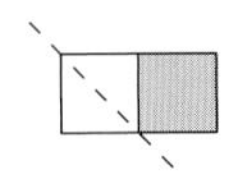 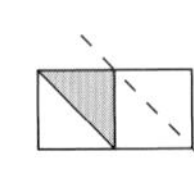 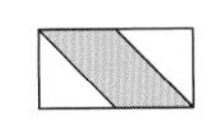

Diagram 2

3. Align a second marked muslin 2½" square with the opposite end of the solid red rectangle (see Diagram 2, again noting the placement of the marked diagonal line). Stitch on the marked line; trim and press as before to make a sashing unit. The pieced sashing unit should measure 2½×4½", including the seam allowances.

4. Repeat steps 1 through 3 to make a total of 273 sashing units.

Assemble the Quilt Center

1. Referring to Diagram 3, lay out 11 blocks and 10 sashing units in a horizontal row. Sew together the pieces to make a block row. Press the seam allowances toward the blocks. The pieced block row should measure 64½×4½", including seam allowances. Repeat to make a total of 13 block rows.

2. Referring to Diagram 4, lay out 11 sashing units and 10 solid red 2½" squares in a horizontal row. Sew together the pieces to make a sashing row. Press the seam allowances toward the solid red squares. The pieced sashing row should measure 64½×2½", including seam allowances. Repeat to make a total of 13 sashing rows.

3. Referring to the photograph *opposite*, lay out the pieced rows, alternating block rows with sashing rows.

4. Sew together the rows to make the quilt center. Press the seam allowances in one direction. The pieced quilt center should measure 64½×78½", including the seam allowances.

Add the Border

1. Cut and piece the muslin 2×42" strips to make the following:
   - 2—2×78½" border strips
   - 2—2×67½" border strips

2. Sew the long muslin border strips to the long edges of the pieced quilt center. Then add the short muslin border strips to the short edges of the pieced quilt center to complete the quilt top. Press all seam allowances toward the muslin border.

Complete the Quilt

1. Layer the quilt top, batting, and backing according to the instructions in Quilter's Schoolhouse, which begins on *page 150*. Quilt as desired.

2. Use the solid red 2½×42" strips to bind the quilt according to the instructions in Quilter's Schoolhouse.

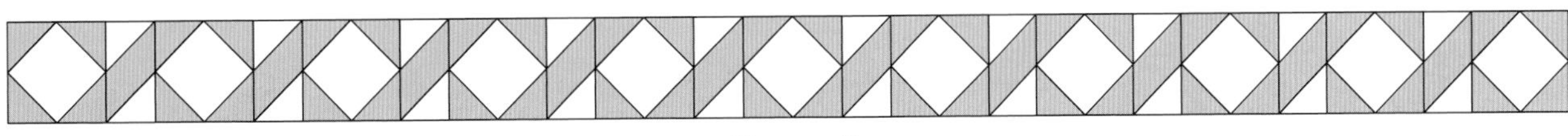

Diagram 3

Diagram 4

continued

Pinwheel Swirl Quilt

optional sizes

If you'd like to make this quilt in a size other than for a twin bed, use the information *below.*

Alternate quilt sizes	Crib/Lap	Full/Queen	King
Number of blocks	63	224	324
Number of sashing units	117	432	630
Number of sashing squares	54	208	306
Number of blocks wide by long	7×9	14×16	18×18
Finished size	43×57"	85×99"	109×111"
Yardage requirements			
Muslin	2½ yards	6⅔ yards	9 yards
Solid red	3 yards	8¼ yards	11⅝ yards
Backing	2¾ yards	7⅝ yards	9⅝ yards
Batting	49×63"	91×105"	115×117"

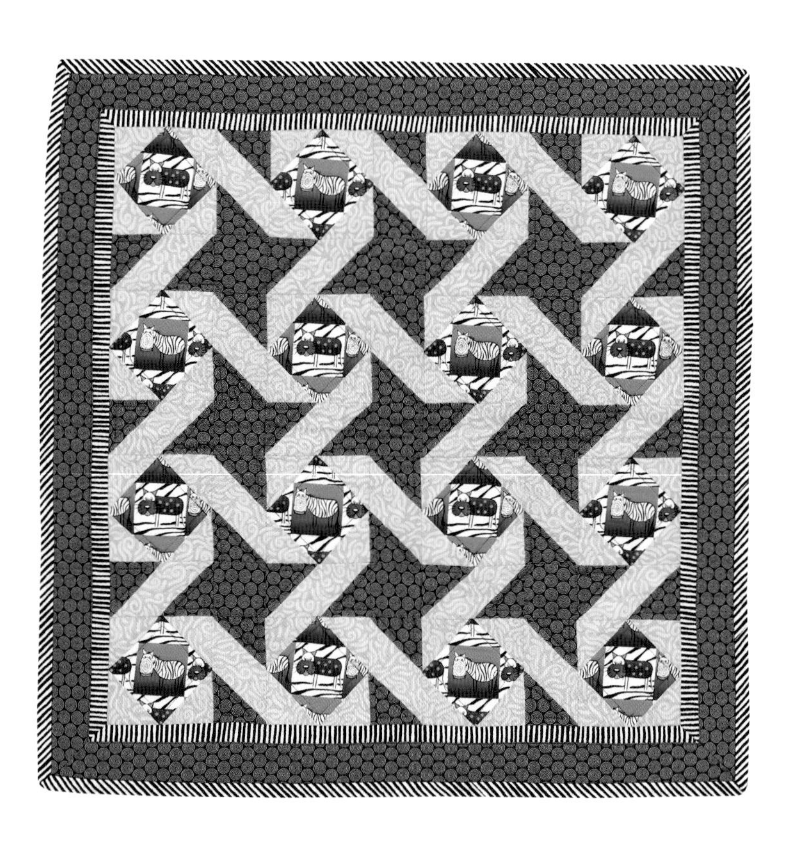

KID'S QUILT

Fussy-cut an animal print and feature it in this lighthearted wall hanging.

Materials

½ yard of zebra print for blocks

⅝ yard of green print for blocks and sashing

⅔ yard of blue print for blocks, sashing, and outer border

¾ yard of black-and-white stripe for inner border and binding

1 yard of backing fabric

33" square of quilt batting

Finished quilt top: 26¾" square

Cut the Fabrics

To make the best use of your fabrics, cut the pieces in the order that follows. Isolating and cutting out a specific print motif is called fussy cutting. For the block centers, cut a 3⅜" square template from transparent template plastic and lay it on the zebra print to determine which portion you want to include. Mark the template placement with pins or chalk to make sure motifs align consistently within the squares.

From zebra print, cut:
- 16—3⅜" squares

From green print, cut:
- 32—2⅞" squares, cutting each in half diagonally for a total of 64 triangles
- 24—2½×4½" rectangles

From blue print, cut:
- 4—2¼×30" outer border strips
- 57—2½" squares

From black-and-white stripe, cut:
- 1—18×30" rectangle, cutting it into enough 4"-wide bias strips to total 115" in length (For specific instructions, see Cutting Bias Strips in Quilter's Schoolhouse, which begins on *page 150.*)
- 4—1⅛×25" inner border strips

Assemble the Blocks

Referring to Assemble the Blocks on *page 9*, steps 1 and 2, use four green print triangles and one zebra print 3⅜" square to make a Diamond in the Square block. Repeat to make a total of 16 Diamond in the Square blocks.

Assemble the Sashing Units

Referring to Assemble the Sashing Units on *page 11*, steps 1 through 3, use two blue print 2½" squares and one green print 2½×4½" rectangle to make a sashing unit. Repeat to make a total of 24 sashing units.

Assemble the Quilt Center

1. Referring to the photograph *opposite* for placement, lay out the blocks, sashing units, and nine blue print 2½" squares in seven horizontal rows.

2. Sew together the pieces in each row. Press the seam allowances toward the blocks and the blue print squares. Then join the rows to make the quilt center. Press the seam allowances in one direction. The pieced quilt center should measure 22½" square, including the seam allowances.

Add the Borders

1. With midpoints aligned, sew the black-and-white stripe 1⅛×25" inner border strips to opposite edges of the quilt center, beginning and ending the seams ¼" from the corners. Add the remaining black-and-white stripe 1⅛×25" inner border strips to the remaining edges of the quilt center, mitering the corners. For information on mitering corners, see Mitered Border Corners in Quilter's Schoolhouse, which begins on *page 150.* Press all the seam allowances toward the inner border.

2. As in Step 1, sew the blue print 2¼×30" outer border strips to the quilt center edges, mitering the corners. Press the seam allowances toward the outer border.

Complete the Quilt

1. Layer the quilt top, batting, and backing according to instructions in Quilter's Schoolhouse, which begins on *page 150.* Quilt as desired.

2. Use a ⅝" seam allowance and the black-and-white stripe 4"-wide bias strips to bind the quilt according to the instructions in Quilter's Schoolhouse.

WALL HANGING

Color cascades across this two-block quilt for a dramatic finish to accent your decor.

Materials

4 yards total of assorted batiks in yellow, orange, magenta, purple, blue, indigo, and black for blocks, sashing, and binding

2⅝ yards of backing fabric

52×46" of quilt batting

Finished quilt top: 46×40"

Cut the Fabrics

To make the best use of your fabrics, lay them out on a table from the lightest yellow to black. Cut the pieces in the order that follows, using the Quilt Assembly Diagram *opposite* to guide your choices. If possible, arrange the pieces on a design wall as you cut them out.

From assorted batiks, cut:

- 56—3⅜" squares
- 97—2½×4½" rectangles
- 112—2⅞" squares, cutting each in half diagonally for a total of 224 triangles
- 236—2½" squares
- Enough 2½"-wide pieces in lengths varying from 12" to 36" to total 185" in length for binding

Assemble the Blocks

1. Referring to Assemble the Blocks on *page 9*, steps 1 and 2, use four yellow batik triangles and one yellow batik 3⅜" square to make a Diamond in the Square block.

2. Repeat Step 1 using the remaining batik triangles and 3⅜" squares to make a total of 56 Diamond in the Square blocks.

Assemble the Sashing Units

1. Referring to Assemble the Sashing Units on *page 11*, steps 1 through 3, use two yellow batik 2½" squares and one yellow batik 2½×4½" rectangle to make a sashing unit.

2. Repeat Step 1 using batik 2½" squares and 2½×4½" rectangles to make 97 sashing units.

Assemble the Quilt Top

1. Referring to the photograph *opposite* and the Quilt Assembly Diagram for placement, lay out the blocks, sashing units, and remaining assorted batik 2½" squares in 13 horizontal rows.

2. Sew together the pieces in each row. Press the seam allowances toward the blocks and 2½" squares. Then join the rows to make the quilt top. Press the seam allowances in one direction.

Complete the Quilt

1. Layer the quilt top, batting, and backing according to instructions in Quilter's Schoolhouse, which begins on *page 150*. Quilt as desired.

2. Piece the assorted yellow to black print 2½"-wide pieces into a single 185"-long strip. Use the strip to bind the quilt according to the instructions in Quilter's Schoolhouse, aligning the colors in the binding with the colors in the quilt top.

Quilt Assembly Diagram

Many Trips AROUND THE WORLD

A simple square reaches new heights of grandeur in this antique quilt. With more than 5,200 pieces, the quilt stands as a testament to the quiltmaker's masterful color placement and seemingly monumental patience.

Materials

7 yards total of assorted print scraps for squares

2 yards of solid orange for squares and binding

4¾ yards of backing fabric

73×85" of quilt batting

Finished quilt top: 67×79"

Quantities specified for 44/45"-wide, 100% cotton fabrics. All measurements include a ¼" seam allowance. Sew with right sides together unless otherwise stated.

Cut the Fabrics

To make the best use of your fabrics, cut the pieces in the order that follows. Note that the featured quilt's pattern is one of concentric squares—bands of 4, 8, 12, 16, 20, and 24 squares around a single center square. In every case, the final square of 24 is orange. To duplicate this look, cut your squares accordingly.

continued

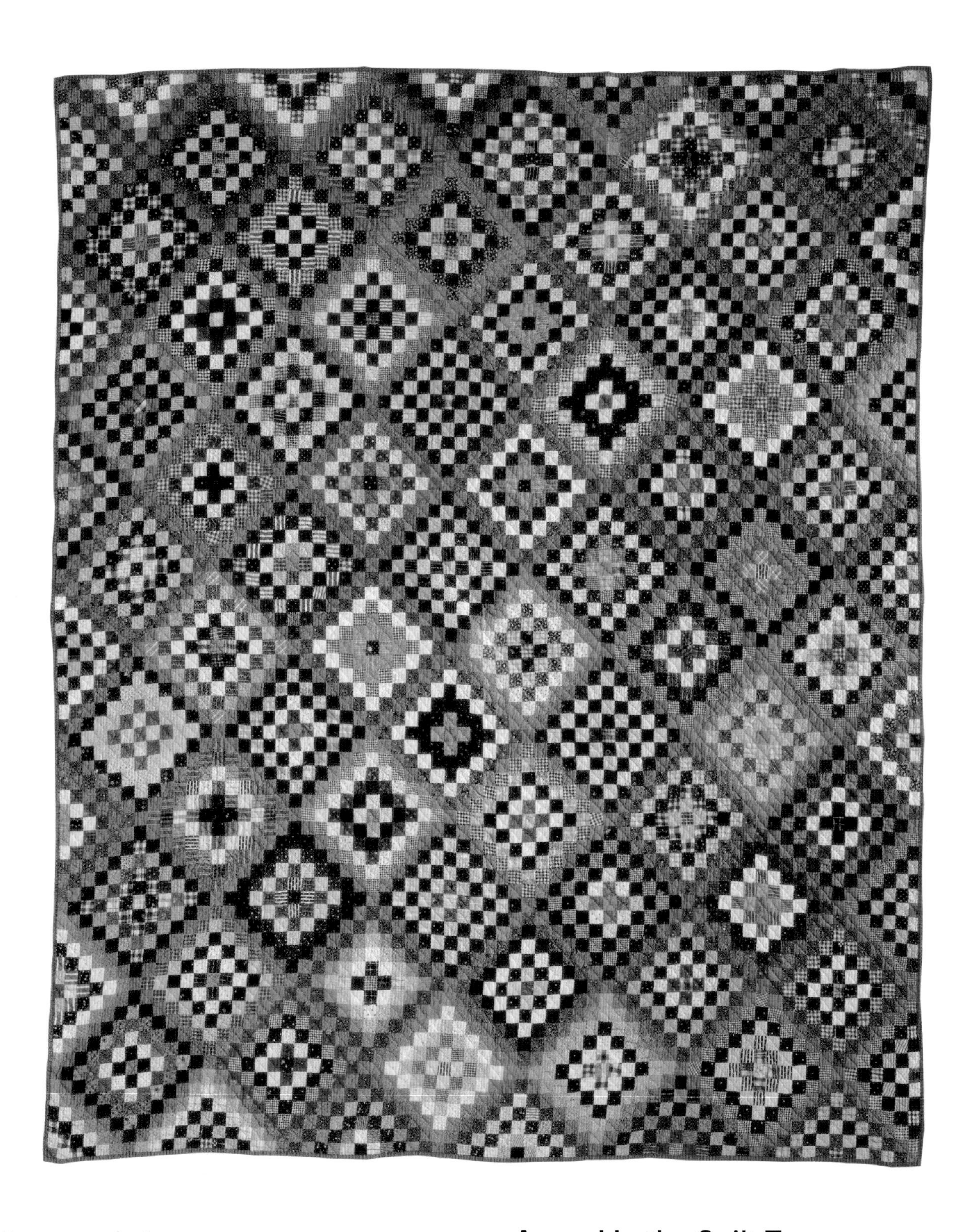

From assorted print scraps, cut:
- 4,494—1½" squares

From solid orange, cut:
- 8—2½×42" binding strips
- 799—1½" squares

Assemble the Quilt Top

1. Referring to the Quilt Assembly Diagram and the photograph *above* for placement, lay out the solid orange 1½" squares and the assorted print 1½" squares in 79 horizontal rows of 67 squares each. Sew together the squares in each row. Press the seam allowances in one direction, alternating the direction with each row.

2. Join the rows to complete the quilt top. Press the seam allowances in one direction.

Complete the Quilt

1. Layer the quilt top, batting, and backing according to the instructions in Quilter's Schoolhouse, which begins on *page 150*.

2. Quilt as desired. This antique quilt was hand-quilted in diagonal rows that run from upper left to lower right.

3. Use the solid orange 2½×42" strips to bind the quilt according to the instructions in Quilter's Schoolhouse.

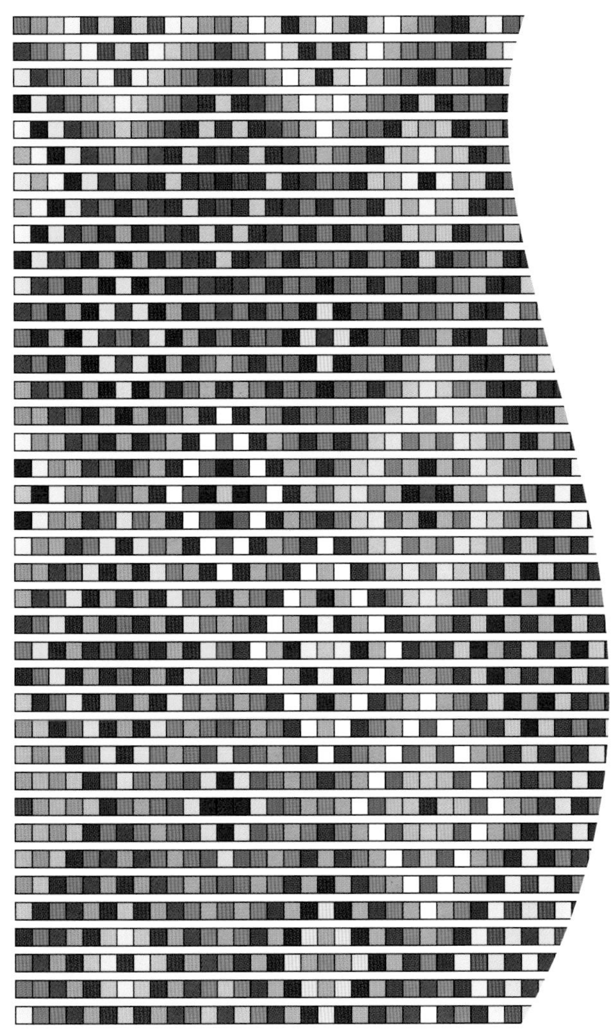

Quilt Assembly Diagram

PICNIC CLOTH

Patriotic colors turn this pattern into a quilt perfect for the 4th of July.

continued

Materials

⅛ yard of red print No. 1 for center squares

⅓ yard of red print No. 2 for squares

⅝ yard of red print No. 3 for squares

¾ yard of blue print No. 1 for squares

1 yard of blue print No. 2 for squares

1⅛ yards of blue print No. 3 for squares

1⅛ yards of dark blue print for squares and binding

3⅛ yards of backing fabric

55" square of quilt batting

Finished quilt top: 49" square

Cut the Fabrics

To make the best use of your fabrics, cut the pieces in the order that follows. Note that the featured quilt's pattern is one of concentric squares—bands of 4, 8, 12, 16, 20, and 24 squares around a single center square. In every case, the final square of 24 is dark blue. To duplicate this look, cut your squares accordingly.

From red print No. 1, cut:
- 41—1½" squares

From red print No. 2, cut:
- 144—1½" squares

From red print No. 3, cut:
- 272—1½" squares

From blue print No. 1, cut:
- 400—1½" squares

From blue print No. 2, cut:
- 528—1½" squares

From blue print No. 3, cut:
- 656—1½" squares

From dark blue print, cut:
- 6—2½×42" binding strips
- 360—1½" squares

Assemble the Quilt Top

1. Referring to the Quilt Assembly Diagram and the photograph *opposite* for placement, lay out the 1½" squares in 49 horizontal rows of 49 squares each. Sew together the squares in each row. Press the seam allowances in one direction, alternating the direction with each row.
2. Join the rows to complete the quilt top. Press the seam allowances in one direction.

Complete the Quilt

1. Layer the quilt top, batting, and backing according to instructions in Quilter's Schoolhouse, which begins on *page 150*. Quilt as desired.
2. Use the dark blue print 2½×42" strips to bind the quilt according to the instructions in Quilter's Schoolhouse.

Quilt Assembly Diagram

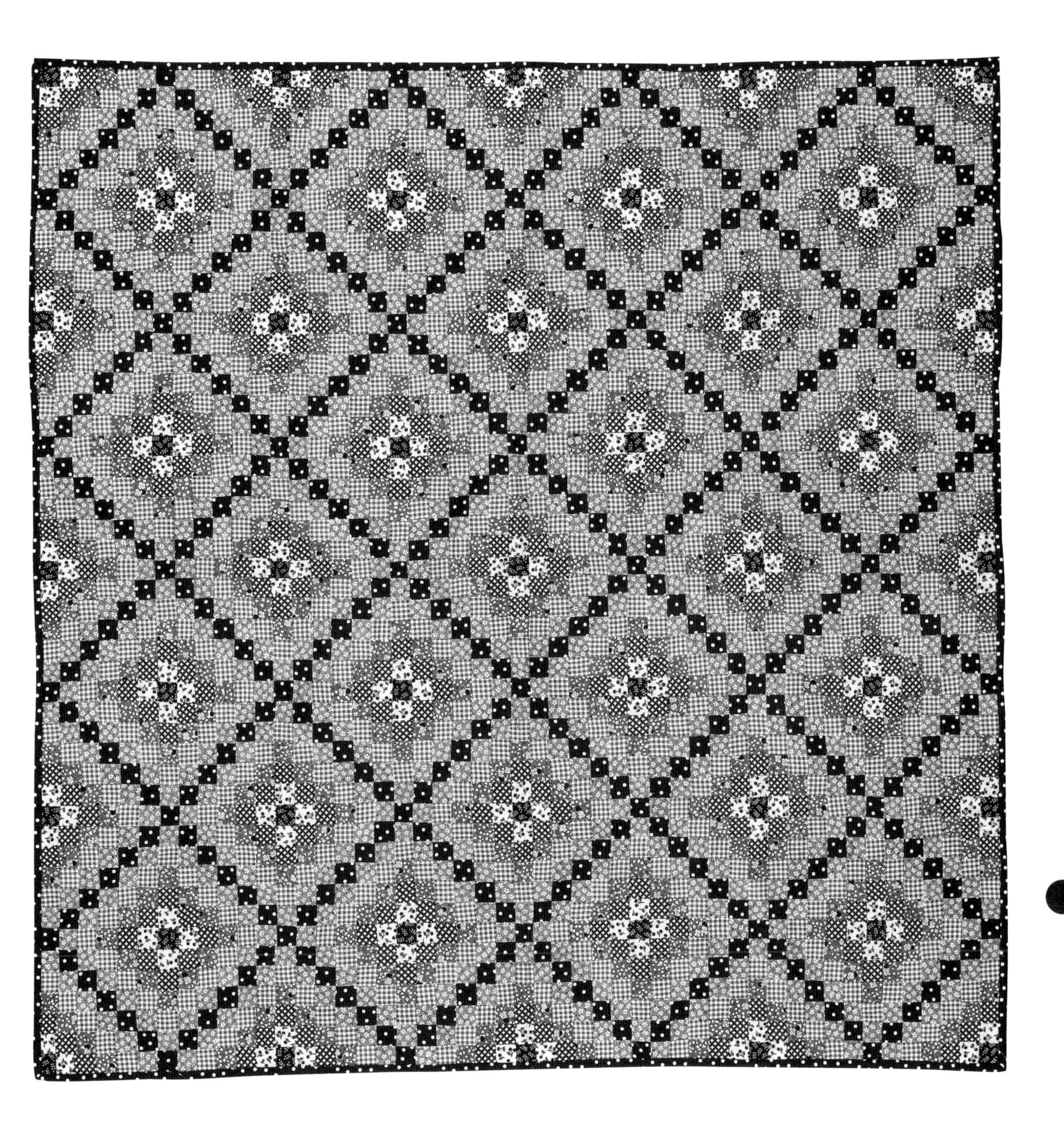

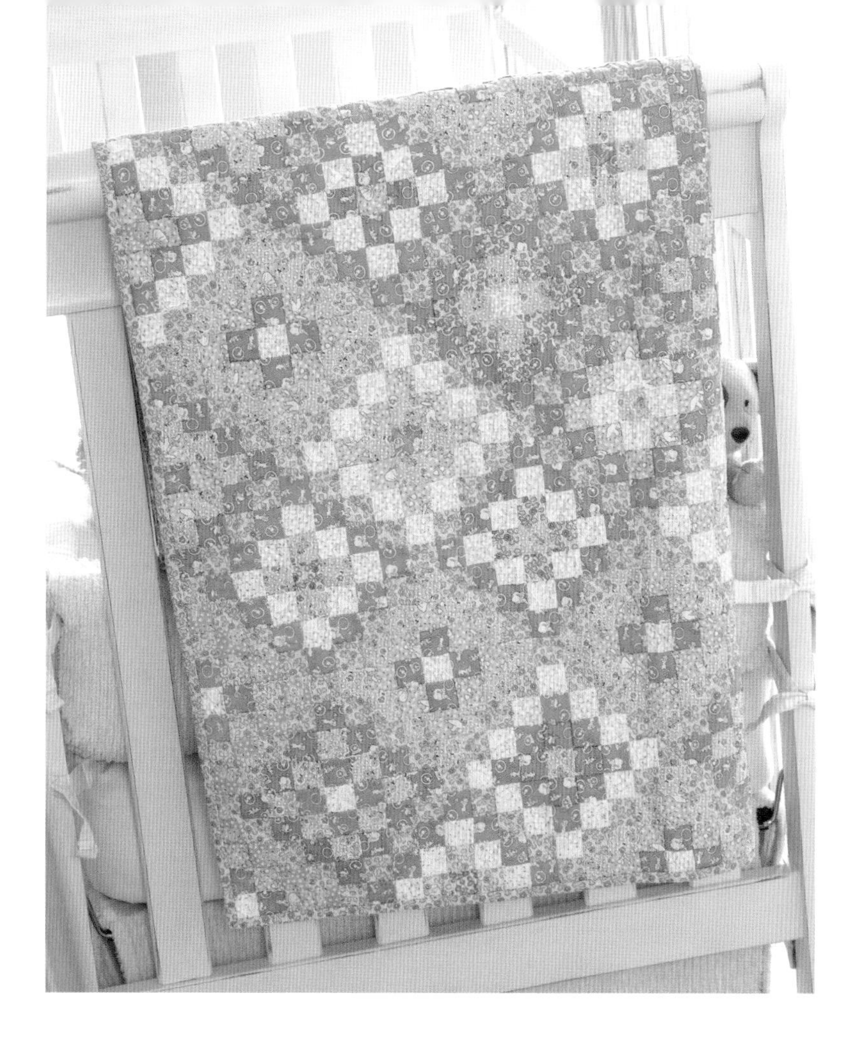

BABY QUILT

Intricate piecing adds texture to this quilt and allows you to use a variety of fabrics.

Materials

2¼ yards total of assorted pastel print scraps for squares

1⅛ yards of green print for squares and binding

1⅝ yards of backing fabric

39×55" of quilt batting

Finished quilt top: 33×49"

Cut the Fabrics

To make the best use of your fabrics, cut the pieces in the order that follows. Note that the featured quilt's pattern is one of concentric squares—bands of 4, 8, 12, and 16 squares around a single center square. In every case, the final square of 16 is green. To duplicate this look, cut your squares accordingly.

From assorted pastel print scraps, cut:
- 1,272—1½" squares

From green print, cut:
- 5—2½×42" binding strips
- 346—1½" squares

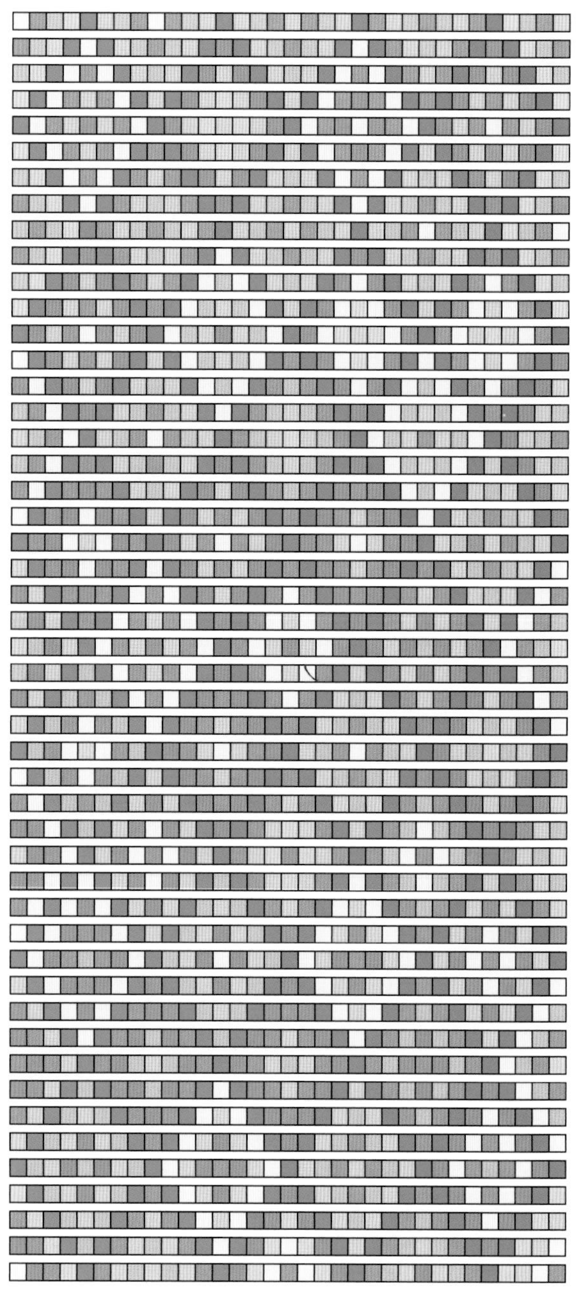

Quilt Assembly Diagram

Assemble the Quilt Top

1. Referring to the Quilt Assembly Diagram and photograph *above* for placement, lay out the green print 1½" squares and the assorted pastel print 1½" squares in 49 horizontal rows of 33 squares each. Sew together the squares in each row. Press the seam allowances in one direction, alternating the direction with each row.

2. Join the rows to complete the quilt top. Press the seam allowances in one direction.

Complete the Quilt

1. Layer the quilt top, batting, and backing according to instructions in Quilter's Schoolhouse, which begins on *page 150*. Quilt as desired.

2. Use the green print 2½×42" strips to bind the quilt according to the instructions in Quilter's Schoolhouse.

TURKEY *Tracks*

The maker of this antique appliquéd quilt set Turkey Tracks blocks on point, turning them into fresh spring buds about to burst into blossom. Needle-turn appliqué simplifies the process of re-creating the quilt.

Materials

- 2½ yards of dark pink print for appliqués
- 1½ yards of solid green for appliqués
- 3¼ yards of muslin for appliqué foundations and inner border
- 3⅜ yards of light pink print for setting squares, setting triangles, corner triangles, and outer border
- ⅔ yard of solid pink for binding
- 5⅛ yards of backing fabric
- 77×92" of quilt batting
- Freezer paper
- Dry-mount adhesive

Finished quilt top: 70½×85⅜"
Finished block: 10½" square

Quantities specified for 44/45"-wide, 100% cotton fabrics. All measurements include a ¼" seam allowance. Sew with right sides together unless otherwise stated.

Cut the Fabrics

To make the best use of your fabrics, cut the pieces in the order that follows. The setting and corner triangles are cut larger than necessary; they will be trimmed before the borders are added.

The patterns are on *Pattern Sheet 2*. To make templates of the patterns, follow the instructions in Quilter's Schoolhouse, which begins on *page 150*.

continued

From dark pink print, cut:
- 20—11" squares for appliqués

From solid green, cut:
- 80—4×5½" rectangles for appliqués

From muslin, cut:
- 7—3×42" strips for inner border
- 20—11½" squares for appliqué foundations

From light pink print, cut:
- 8—3½×42" strips for outer border
- 4—16½" squares, cutting each diagonally twice in an X for a total of 16 setting triangles (you'll have 2 leftover triangles)
- 12—11" squares for setting squares
- 2—9" squares, cutting each in half diagonally for a total of 4 corner triangles

From solid pink, cut:
- 8—2½×42" binding strips

From freezer paper, cut:
- 20—11½" squares
- 80—4×5½" rectangles

Cut and Prepare the Appliqué Pieces

The following instructions are for a freezer-paper template, needle-turn appliqué method. The freezer-paper templates form a base around which the fabrics are shaped.

1. Fold a freezer-paper 11½" square in half horizontally, making a rectangle (see Diagram 1). Fold the freezer-paper rectangle in half, making a 5¾" square. Staple the square in a corner to keep the folds stable.

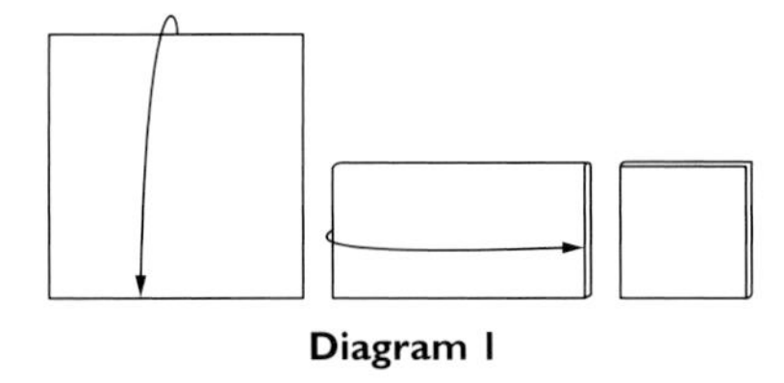

Diagram 1

2. Position Pattern A on the folded freezer paper as shown in Diagram 2. Tape the pattern securely to the folded freezer paper. (A dry-mount adhesive is recommended because it allows the pattern to be removed and reused.)

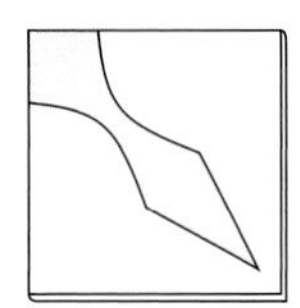

Diagram 2

3. Cut the freezer paper along the pattern edges to make a template; do not add any seam allowances or extensions. Remove the pattern.

4. Carefully unfold the freezer-paper template. Position it, shiny side down, on the wrong side of a dark pink print 11" square.

5. Press the freezer-paper template in place with a hot, dry iron. Lift the iron after five seconds and check to be sure that the template has completely adhered to the fabric.

6. Cut the fabric about 3/16" beyond the freezer-paper edges to make an appliqué shape. Clip any inside curves or points as necessary; do not clip outside curves.

7. Repeat steps 1 through 6 to make a total of 20 dark pink print A shapes.

8. Trace Pattern B onto the paper side of the 80 freezer paper 4×5½" rectangles; do not add any seam allowances or extensions. Cut out along the pattern edges to make 80 templates.

9. Position each freezer-paper template, shiny side down, on the wrong side of a solid green 4×5½" rectangle.

10. Press each freezer-paper template in place with a hot, dry iron. Lift the iron after five seconds and check to be sure that the template has completely adhered to the fabric.

11. Cut the fabric about 3/16" beyond the freezer-paper edges to make appliqué shapes. Clip the inside curves or points on the appliqué shapes where necessary; do not clip outside curves.

Appliqué the Blocks

1. Fold a muslin 11½" square appliqué foundation in half diagonally in both directions. Lightly finger-crease to create positioning guides for the appliqué shapes; unfold.

2. Pin a dark pink print A appliqué shape and four solid green B appliqué shapes in place on the muslin foundation.

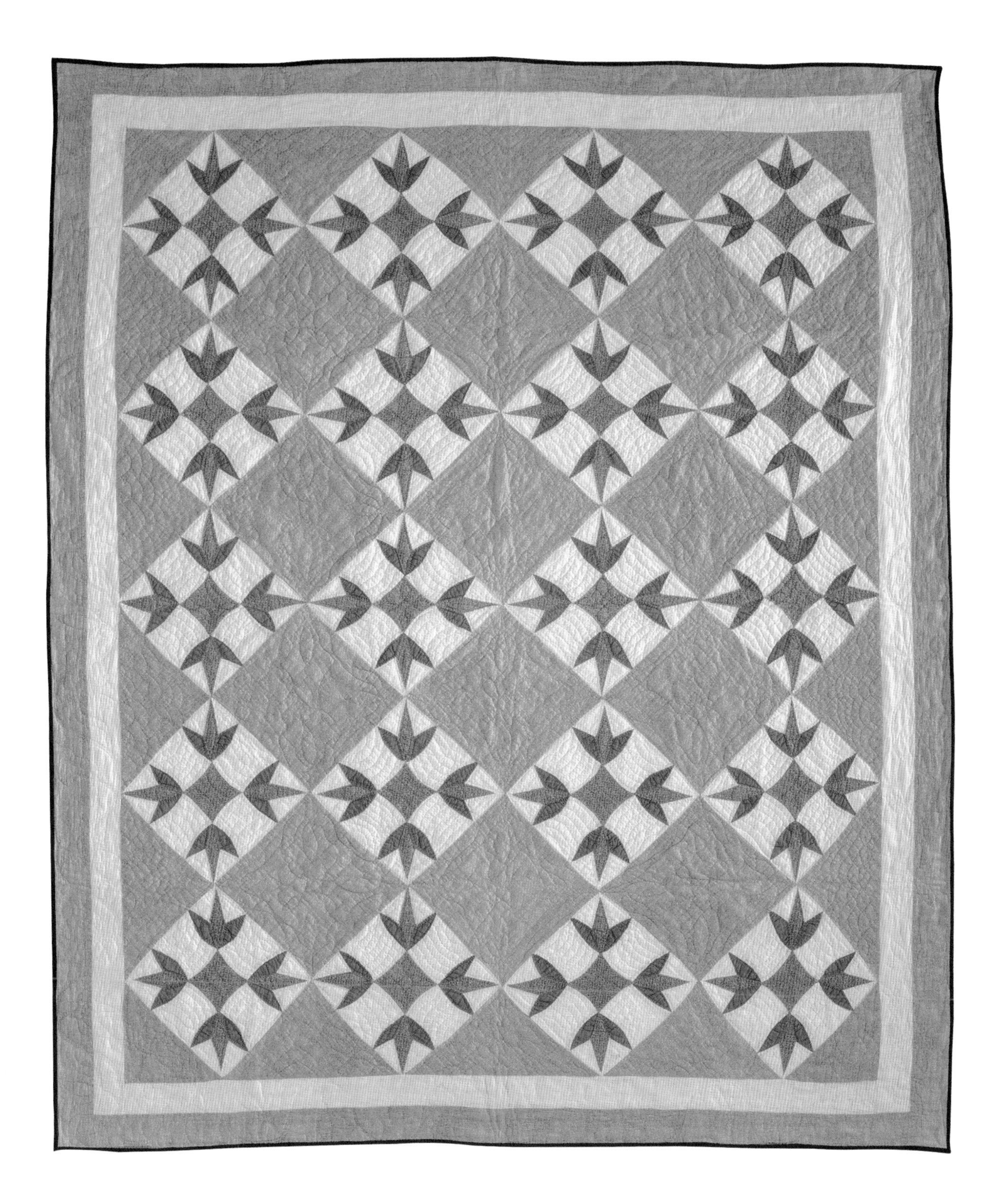

3. Using green thread, needle-turn appliqué the solid green B shapes to the muslin foundation, leaving a ½" opening in each. Using each opening, slide your needle between the green shapes and freezer paper. Gently loosen the freezer-paper templates and pull them out. Stitch the openings closed.

4. Appliqué the dark pink print A shape to the muslin foundation, leaving a ½" opening along one edge. Remove the freezer-paper template as before and stitch the opening closed. Gently press the appliquéd block from the back.

continued

5. Repeat steps 1 through 4 to appliqué a total of 20 blocks. Trim each block to measure 11" square, including the seam allowances.

Assemble the Quilt Center

1. Referring to the photograph on *page 27*, lay out the 20 appliquéd blocks, the 12 light pink print 11" setting squares, and 14 light pink print setting triangles in diagonal rows.

2. Sew together the pieces in each row. Press the seam allowances in one direction, alternating the direction with each row. Then join the rows. Press the seam allowances in one direction. Add the four light pink print corner triangles to make the quilt center.

3. Trim the quilt center, leaving a ¼" seam allowance beyond the block corners. The pieced quilt center should measure 60×74⅞", including the seam allowances.

Add the Borders

1. Cut and piece the muslin 3×42" strips to make the following:
   - 2—3×79⅞" inner border strips
   - 2—3×60" inner border strips

2. Sew the short muslin inner border strips to the short edges of the pieced quilt center. Then add the long muslin inner border strips to the long edges of the pieced quilt center. Press the seam allowances toward the inner border.

3. Cut and piece the light pink print 3½×42" strips to make the following:
   - 2—3½×85⅞" outer border strips
   - 2—3½×65" outer border strips

4. Sew the short light pink print outer border strips to the short edges of the pieced quilt center. Then add the long light pink print outer border strips to the long edges of the pieced quilt center to complete the quilt top. Press the seam allowances toward the outer border.

Complete the Quilt

1. Layer the quilt top, batting, and backing according to the instructions in Quilter's Schoolhouse, which begins on *page 150*. Quilt as desired.

2. Use the solid pink 2½×42" strips to bind the quilt according to the instructions in Quilter's Schoolhouse.

Turkey Tracks Quilt
optional sizes

If you'd like to make this quilt in a size other than for a twin bed, use the information *below*.

Alternate quilt sizes	Crib/Lap	Full/Queen	King
Number of blocks	9	30	36
Number of blocks wide by long	3×3	5×6	6×6
Finished size	55⅝" square	85⅜×100¼"	100¼" square
Yardage requirements			
Dark pink print	1⅓ yards	3½ yards	4⅛ yards
Solid green	¾ yard	2⅛ yards	2½ yards
Muslin	1⅞ yards	4⅜ yards	5¼ yards
Light pink print	2½ yards	6 yards	6½ yards
Solid pink	⅝ yard	⅞ yard	⅞ yard
Backing	3½ yards	7⅔ yards	9 yards
Batting	62" square	92×107"	107" square

BED QUILT

Black fabric sets off the striped appliqués that strut across this bold piece.

Materials

72—11" squares (7⅞ yards total) of assorted stripes for appliqués

8⅛ yards of solid black for appliqué foundations

⅞ yard of dark stripe for binding

7½ yards of backing fabric

90×101" of quilt batting

23 yards of lightweight fusible web

Finished quilt top: 84×94½"

continued

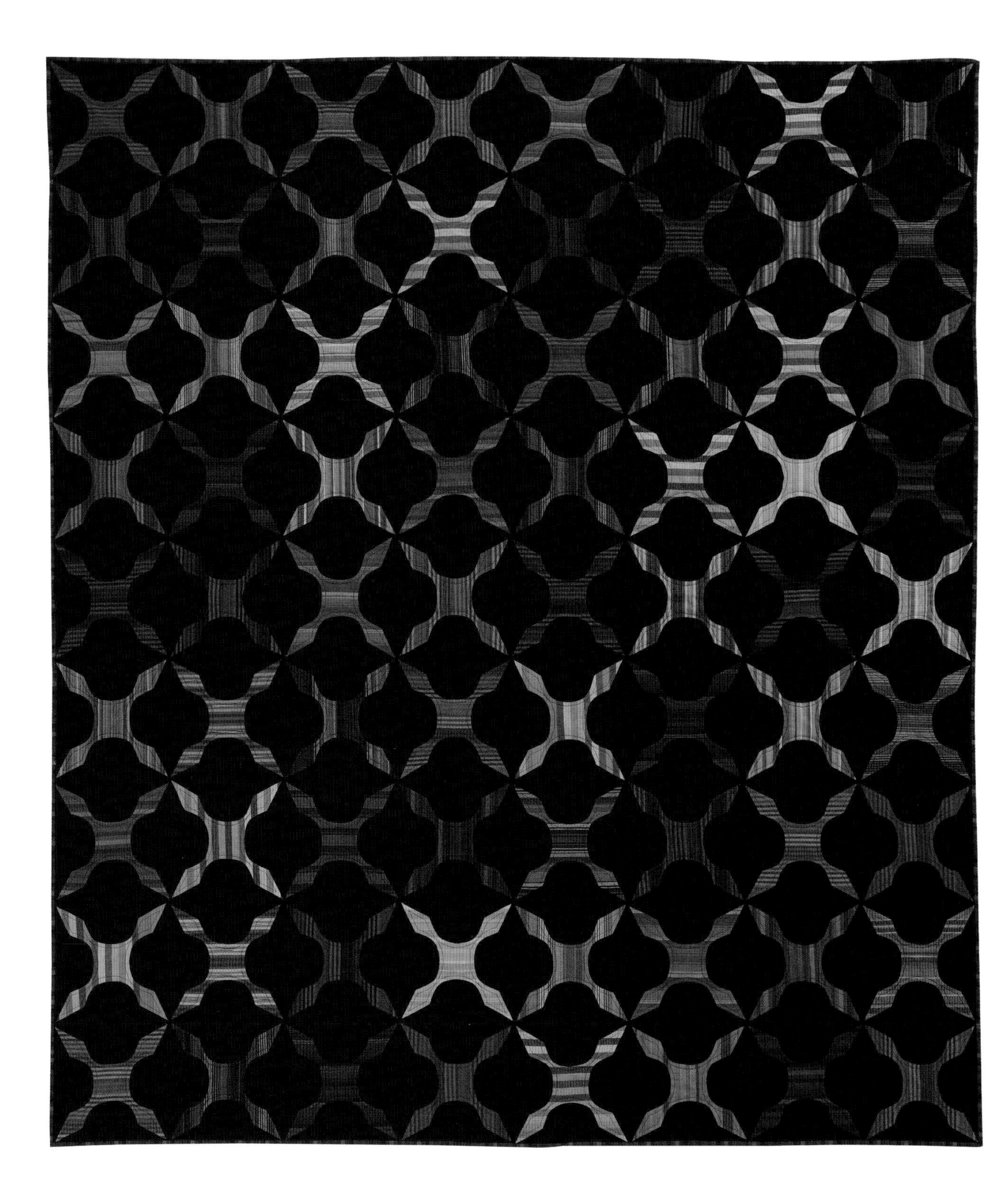

Cut the Fabrics

To make the best use of your fabrics, cut the pieces in the order that follows. This project uses "Turkey Tracks" Pattern A, which is on *Pattern Sheet 2.*

To use fusible web for appliquéing, as was done in this project, follow these steps.

1. Make a template for the appliqué shape by tracing Pattern A four times, rotating the pattern at the dashed fold lines to form a square in the center.

2. Lay the fusible web, paper side up, over the Pattern A template. With a pencil, trace the

pattern 72 times, leaving ½" between tracings. Cut out each fusible-web shape roughly ¼" outside the traced lines.

2. Following the manufacturer's instructions, press the fusible-web shapes onto the backs of the assorted stripe 11" squares; let cool. Cut out the fabric shapes on the drawn lines. Peel off the paper backings.

From solid black, cut:
- 72—11½" squares for appliqué foundations

From dark stripe, cut:
- 10—2½×42" binding strips

Appliqué the Blocks

1. Referring to Appliqué the Blocks on *page 26*, Step 1, prepare a solid black appliqué foundation square.

2. Fuse a stripe A shape to the solid black foundation square. Using invisible thread, machine-appliqué the shape in place to make an appliquéd block.

3. Repeat steps 1 and 2 to appliqué a total of 72 blocks. Trim each block to measure 11" square, including the seam allowances.

Assemble the Quilt Top

1. Referring to the photograph *opposite*, lay out the 72 appliquéd blocks in nine horizontal rows.

2. Sew together the blocks in each row. Press the seam allowances in one direction, alternating the direction with each row. Then join the rows to make the quilt top. Press the seam allowances in one direction.

Complete the Quilt

1. Layer the quilt top, batting, and backing according to the instructions in Quilter's Schoolhouse, which begins on *page 150*. Quilt as desired.

2. Use the dark stripe 2½×42" strips to bind the quilt according to the instructions in Quilter's Schoolhouse.

WALL HANGING

Bold colors add punch to a four-block version of this classic pattern.

continued

Materials

4—11" squares of assorted yellow-and-orange prints for appliqués

4—⅛-yard pieces of assorted green prints for appliqués

¾ yard of purple print for appliqué foundations

⅞ yard of green floral for setting square, setting triangles, and corner triangles

½ yard of red print for inner border

½ yard of multicolor print for outer border

¼ yard of yellow print for piping

½ yard of purple floral for binding

2⅝ yards of backing fabric

47" square of quilt batting

1¾ yards of lightweight fusible web

Finished quilt top: 40¾" square

Cut the Fabrics

To make the best use of your fabrics, cut the pieces in the order that follows. This project uses "Turkey Tracks" patterns, which are on *Pattern Sheet 2.*

To use fusible web for appliquéing, as was done in this project, follow these steps.

1. Lay the fusible web, paper side up, over Pattern A. With a pencil, trace the pattern four times, leaving ½" between tracings. Cut out each fusible-web A shape roughly ¼" outside the traced lines.

2. Following the manufacturer's instructions, press the fusible-web A shapes onto the backs of the assorted yellow-and-orange prints; let cool. Cut out the fabric shapes on the drawn lines. Peel off the paper backings.

3. Repeat Step 1 using Pattern B, tracing the pattern 16 times. Press the fusible-web B shapes onto the backs of the assorted green prints; let cool. Cut out the fabric shapes on the drawn lines. Peel off the paper backings.

From purple print, cut:
- 4—11½" squares for appliqué foundations

From green floral, cut:
- 1—16½" square, cutting it diagonally twice in an X for a total of 4 setting triangles
- 1—11" setting square
- 2—9" squares, cutting each in half diagonally for a total of 4 corner triangles

From red print, cut:
- 2—3×35¼" inner border strips
- 2—3×30¼" inner border strips

From multicolor print, cut:
- 2—3½×41¼" outer border strips
- 2—3½×35¼" outer border strips

From yellow print, cut:
- 5—1×42" strips for piping

From purple floral, cut:
- 5—2½×42" binding strips

Appliqué the Blocks

1. Referring to Appliqué the Blocks on *page 26,* Step 1, prepare a purple print appliqué foundation square.

2. Fuse four green print B shapes to the purple print foundation. Using green thread, appliqué the shapes in place.

3. Fuse a yellow-and-orange print A shape to the purple print foundation. Using yellow thread, appliqué the shape in place to make an appliquéd block.

4. Repeat steps 1 through 3 to appliqué a total of four blocks. Trim each block to measure 11" square, including the seam allowances.

Assemble the Quilt Center

1. Referring to the photograph *opposite,* lay out the four appliquéd blocks, the green floral 11" setting square, and the four green floral setting triangles in diagonal rows.

2. Sew together the pieces in each row. Press the seam allowances toward the setting square and setting triangles. Join the rows. Press the seam allowances in one direction. Add the corner triangles to make the quilt center.

3. Trim the quilt center, leaving a ¼" seam allowance beyond the block corners. The pieced quilt center should measure 30¼" square, including the seam allowances.

Add the Borders

1. Sew the red print 3×30¼" inner border strips to opposite edges of the pieced quilt center. Then add the red print 3×35¼" inner border strips to the remaining edges of the pieced quilt center. Press the seam allowances toward the inner border.

2. Sew the multicolor print 3½×35¼" outer border strips to opposite edges of the pieced quilt center. Then add the multicolor print 3½×41¼" outer border strips to the remaining edges of the pieced quilt center to complete the quilt top. Press the seam allowances toward the outer border.

Complete the Quilt

1. Layer the quilt top, batting, and backing according to the instructions in Quilter's Schoolhouse, which begins on *page 150*. Quilt as desired.

2. Cut and piece the yellow print 1×42" strips to make a 170"-long piping strip.

3. With the wrong side inside, fold and press the yellow print piping strip in half lengthwise. Aligning raw edges and using a ¼" seam, baste the folded strip to the quilt top to make the piping; miter the corners.

4. Use the purple floral 2½×42" strips to bind the quilt according to the instructions in Quilter's Schoolhouse. *Note:* About ⅛" of the yellow piping will show between the quilt top and the binding edge once the binding is turned to the back.

BRIGHT AND COLORFUL

Bold, beautiful patterns radiate from these spirited quilts. Watch as a festive "Mississippi Wheel of Fortune" transforms into a rich table topper and then zooms into a race car quilt's sashing. Marvel as "Sunrise, Sunset" tries on crisp blue and white and then breaks into four framed pieces representing the sun's descent. Observe a contemporary "Bali Ho" split apart by star sashing, then covering a large pillow. Approach your next bright quilt with gusto and see what transpires.

Mississippi Wheel of Fortune

A mélange of colorful fabrics mingles with bright baby rickrack to create a whirlwind of movement on designer Karen Stone's foundation-pieced quilt.

Materials

4—18×22" pieces (fat quarters) *each* of red, orange, yellow, green, turquoise, violet, and black prints for blocks and sashing

5/8 yard of black print for binding

4-1/8 yards of backing fabric

74" square of quilt batting

16 yards total of assorted baby rickrack

Finished quilt top: 68" square
Finished block: 12" square

Quantities specified for 44/45"-wide, 100% cotton fabrics. All measurements include a 1/4" seam allowance. Sew with right sides together unless otherwise stated.

Designer Notes

"This is a true scrap quilt, where things get really mixed up and there is not a particular place for any color," designer Karen Stone says of "Mississippi Wheel of Fortune." Her quilt started with a handful of favorite fabrics and grew from there.

"But it could be made with every block the same, or with more controlled colors," she says. "Start with something you love. Then you'll make it work."

Karen used rickrack extensively in this quilt. "I love rickrack and its connection to my grandmother making clothes for me with rickrack on them," she says. "In a quilt, it adds another color, another texture, and more dimension. In this case, I'm using it functionally, too—as a facing in the circles."

continued

Cut the Fabrics

To make the best use of your fabrics, cut the pieces in the order listed in each section. The patterns are on *Pattern Sheet 2.*

Cut and Assemble the Wheel of Fortune Blocks

For each block, designer Karen Stone used seven fabrics (see the detail photograph *below*)—one for the center circle, two for the swirl circle, two for the sawtooth circle, and two for the background square. The cutting and piecing instructions that follow result in one block. Repeat the instructions to make a total of 16 Wheel of Fortune blocks.

From print No. 1 (center circle), cut:
- 1 of Pattern B

From print No. 2 (swirl circle), cut:
- 8 of Pattern A

From print No. 3 (swirl circle), cut:
- 8 of Pattern A

From print No. 4 (sawtooth circle, inside points), cut:
- 16—2½×3" rectangles

From print No. 5 (sawtooth circle, outside points), cut:
- 16—2½×3" rectangles

From print No. 6 (background square), cut:
- 4 of Pattern D

From print No. 7 (background square), cut:
- 4 of Pattern D reversed

1. Pair each print No. 2 A piece with a print No. 3 A piece. Referring to diagrams 1 and 2, sew together one pair. Press the seam allowance toward the convex curve. Sew together each remaining pair. Join the pairs to make a swirl circle (see Diagram 3).

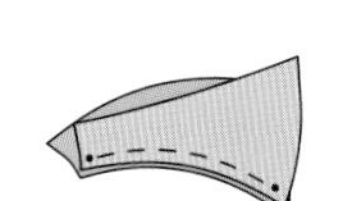

Diagram 1

Diagram 2

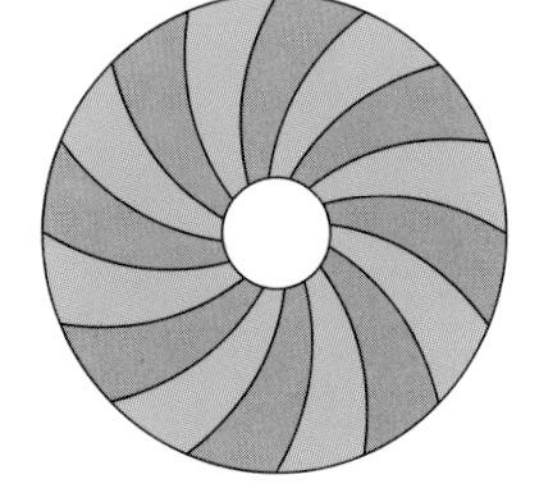

Diagram 3

2. Align a length of baby rickrack with the right side raw edge of the print No. 1 B circle; overlap the rickrack ends slightly. Stitch through the center of the rickrack, using a scant ¼" seam allowance.

3. Press under the B circle seam allowance, pressing the rickrack out, to create the center circle. Half the rickrack should be showing; the other half should be hidden under the B circle (see the detail photograph *below*).

4. Position the center circle over the swirl circle opening (see Diagram 4 and the photograph *above*). Use a straight stitch in the ditch between the edge of the B circle and the rickrack stitching line to hold the center circle in place. Then use a decorative machine stitch and contrasting thread to stitch around the circle a second time.

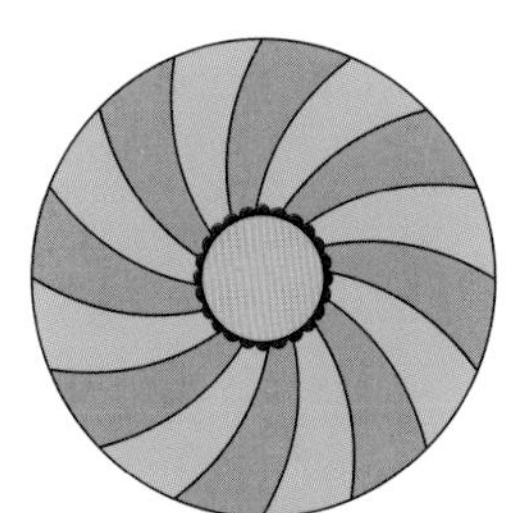

Diagram 4

5. Repeat steps 2 and 3 with a length of baby rickrack and the swirl circle (see the detail photograph *below*).

Make the Foundation Papers

1. With a pencil, trace Pattern C eight times onto tracing paper; include all lines and numbers. Place each tracing on top of a stack of seven blank sheets of tracing paper. (Freezer paper and typing paper also will work.) Staple each stack together once or twice (see Diagram 5).

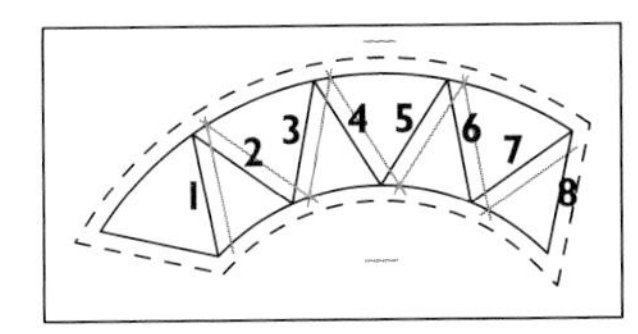

Diagram 5

2. Using a sewing machine set at 10 to 12 stitches per inch with an unthreaded, small-gauge needle, sew on each tracing's inside lines through all layers. Do not stitch on the tracings' outer lines.

3. With your scissors, cut through each stack on the tracing's outer lines to make a total of 64 perforated foundation papers.

Assemble the Sawtooth Circles

In the steps that follow, our print No. 4 (inside points) was a purple print, and our print No. 5 (outside points) was a turquoise print.

1. Layer a turquoise print 2½×3" rectangle atop a purple print 2½×3" rectangle. Put a perforated foundation paper on top of the turquoise rectangle, positioning the rectangles so their aligned edges are a scant ¼" beyond the first stitching line and their top edges extend about ¼" above the top of the arc (see Diagram 6). With the foundation paper on top, sew on stitching line No. 1.

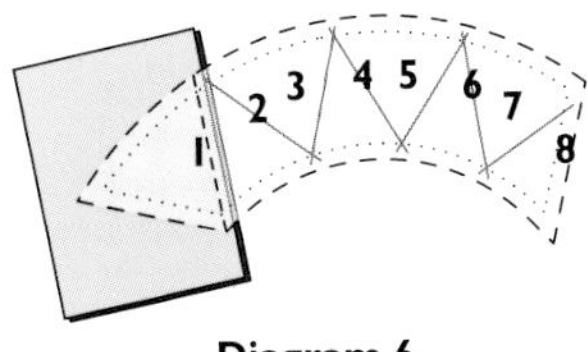

Diagram 6

2. Trim the seam allowance to a scant ¼". Press the rectangles open, pressing the seam allowance toward the purple rectangle. Trim the purple rectangle to a scant ¼" beyond the next stitching line (see Diagram 7). Trim both pieces even with all outer edges of the foundation paper (see Diagram 8).

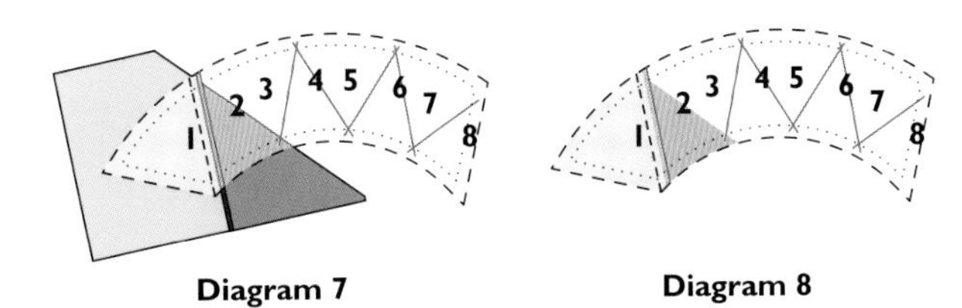

Diagram 7 Diagram 8

3. Position a second turquoise print 2½×3" rectangle under the trimmed purple piece with the right edge a scant ¼" beyond the second stitching line. Sew on stitching line No. 2 as before (see Diagram 9).

Trim the seam allowance if needed. Press the pieces open, pressing the seam allowance toward the turquoise rectangle (see Diagram 10). Trim the second turquoise rectangle to a scant ¼" beyond the next sewing line. Trim the turquoise piece even with the top and bottom edges of the foundation paper.

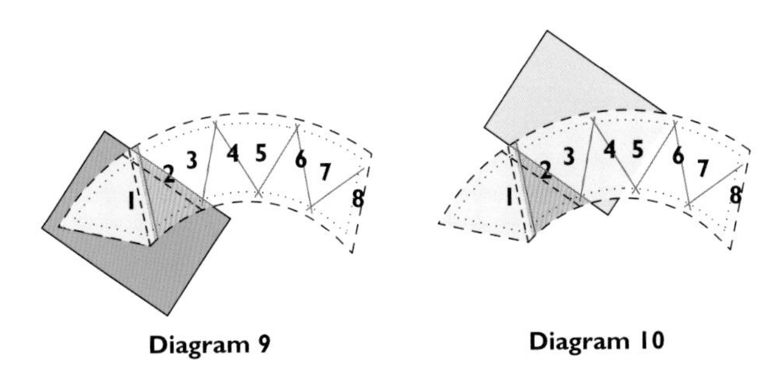

Diagram 9 Diagram 10

4. Continue adding turquoise and purple rectangles to the foundation paper as before until you've pieced the entire arc (see Diagram 11 on *page 40*).

continued

Then, with the blunt edge of a seam ripper, remove the foundation paper.

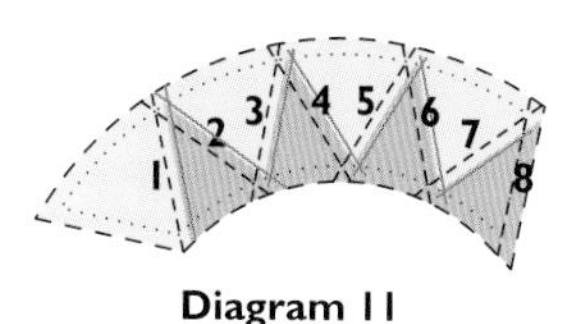

Diagram 11

5. Repeat steps 1 through 4 to make a total of four matching pieced arcs.

6. Sew together the four matching pieced arcs to make a sawtooth circle (see Diagram 12).

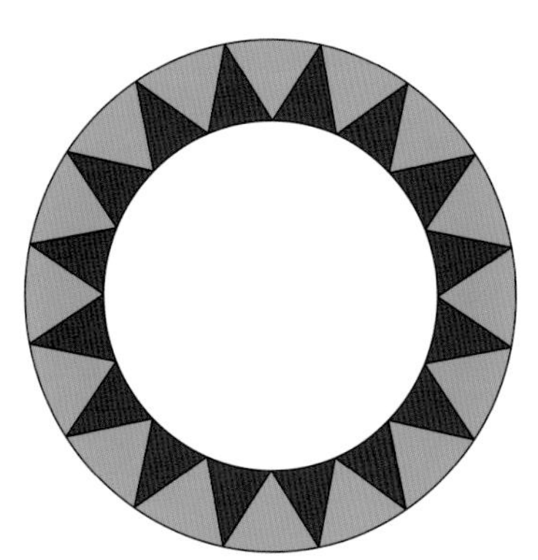
Diagram 12

7. Position the swirl circle atop the opening of the sawtooth circle (see Diagram 13). Use a long straight stitch in the ditch between the edge of the swirl circle and the rickrack stitching line to hold the swirl circle in place. Then use a decorative machine stitch and contrasting thread to stitch around the circle a second time.

Diagram 13

8. Sew together the four print No. 6 D pieces and four print No. 7 D reversed pieces to make a square frame (see Diagram 14). Press the seam allowances open.

Diagram 14

9. Place the sawtooth circle in the square frame opening; join the pieces to complete a block (see Diagram 15). The pieced block should measure 12½" square, including seam allowances.

Diagram 15

Cut and Assemble the Sashing Units

Karen planned the sawtooth sashing units so that each block is surrounded by the same two colors, though not necessarily the same two fabrics. You'll need 16 sets of four matching foundation-pieced strips (Pattern E), plus 16 additional foundation-pieced strips to surround the quilt center. The cutting and piecing instructions that follow result in one sashing unit. Repeat to make a total of 40 sashing units.

continued

From print No. 1, cut:
- 8—2½" squares

From print No. 2, cut:
- 9—2½" squares

From print No. 3, cut:
- 8—2½" squares

From print No. 4, cut:
- 9—2½" squares

From print No. 5, cut:
- 1—1½x12½" strip

1. Following the Make the Foundation Papers instructions on *page 39*, use Pattern E to make a total of 80 perforated foundation papers.

2. In the same manner as assembling the sawtooth circles, use a Pattern E foundation paper, the eight 2½" squares of print No. 1, and the nine 2½" squares of print No. 2 to make a sawtooth sashing strip. Repeat to make a second sawtooth sashing strip using a foundation paper and the 2½" squares from prints Nos. 3 and 4.

3. Referring to the photograph on *page 41* and Diagram 16, sew the two sawtooth sashing strips to the 1½x12½" strip of print No. 5 to make a sashing unit.

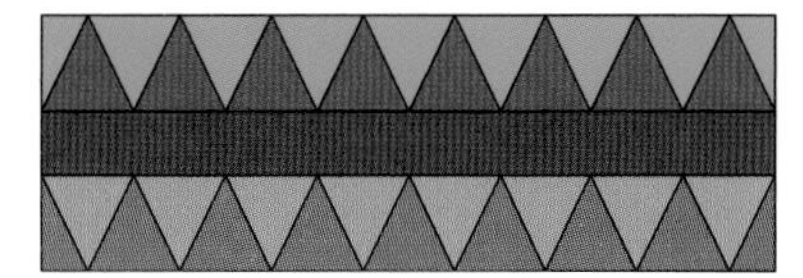

Diagram 16

Cut and Assemble the Sashing Squares

The cutting and piecing instructions that follow are for one sashing square. Repeat to make a total of 25 sashing squares.

From print No. 1, cut:
- 4 of Pattern F

From print No. 2, cut:
- 4 of Pattern G

1. Pair each print No. 1 F piece with a print No. 2 G piece. Referring to diagrams 17 and 18, sew together one pair. Press the seam allowance toward the F piece. Sew together each remaining pair.

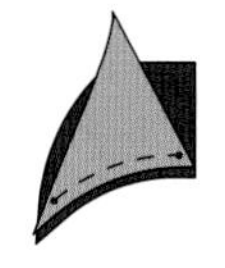

Diagram 17

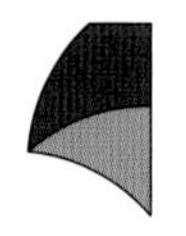

Diagram 18

2. Join the four pairs to make a sashing square (see Diagram 19). Press the seam allowances open. The pieced sashing square should measure 4½" square, including the seam allowances.

Diagram 19

Assemble the Quilt Top

1. Referring to the photograph on *page 41*, lay out the 16 blocks, the 40 sashing units, and the 25 sashing squares in nine horizontal rows.

2. Sew together the pieces in each row. Press the seam allowances toward the blocks or the sashing squares. Then join the rows to complete the quilt top. Press the seam allowances in one direction.

Complete the Quilt

From black print, cut:
- 7—2½x42" binding strips

1. Layer the quilt top, batting, and backing according to the instructions in Quilter's Schoolhouse, which begins on *page 150*.

2. Quilt as desired. Karen machine-quilted straight, curvy, and curly lines in her quilt.

"I like to echo what's going on in the patchwork, so I used a combination of lines," Karen says.

Matching and complementary threads create eye-catching designs—daisies, spirals, arrowheads, and free-form pine trees—on the brightly colored batik, floral, geometric, and polka-dot fabrics. A daisy design emanates from the center of the blocks; a scalloped design spirals around the centers in threads of two colors. Karen repeated these designs in the sashing strips.

"I love busy fabrics, and thread choice can bring interest to a quilt or calm it down," she says.

The threads in this quilt bring texture and movement without competing with the fabrics. When Karen is deciding what to quilt where, she considers the quilt top before the quilt back.

"If it is good on the front, it will be excellent on the back," she says.

She repeated the quilting design in each block, so a symmetry of designs in variegated bobbin thread boldly appears on the plaid backing, creating a movement all its own.

"The variegated thread was just more fun on the back," Karen says.

3. Use the black print 2½×42" strips to bind the quilt according to the instructions in Quilter's Schoolhouse, which begins on *page 150*.

BED QUILT

This quilt's triangle sashing looks like flags waving around a speedy race car print.

Materials

3⅞ yards of race car print for blocks

1¼ yards *each* of solid red, orange, yellow, green, and blue for sashing

⅝ yard of solid white for sashing

7⅝ yards of solid black for sashing

⅞ yard of black-and-white check for binding

7½ yards of backing fabric

90×106" of quilt batting

Finished quilt top: 84×100"

continued

Cut the Fabrics

To make the best use of your fabrics, cut the pieces in the order that follows. This project uses "Mississippi Wheel of Fortune" patterns, which are on *Pattern Sheet 2.* To make templates of the patterns, follow the instructions in Quilter's Schoolhouse, which begins on *page 150.*

From race car print, cut:

- 30—12½" squares

Cut and Assemble the Sashing Units

Refer to Make the Foundation Papers on *page 39,* use Pattern E and make a total of 142 perforated foundation papers. The cutting and piecing instructions that follow result in one red/blue sashing unit. Referring to the photograph *opposite* for color placement, repeat to make a total of 14 red/blue sashing units, 14 red/orange sashing units, 15 blue/green sashing units, 14 yellow/green sashing units, and 14 orange/yellow sashing units.

From solid red, cut:

- 8—2½" squares

From solid blue, cut:

- 8—2½" squares

From solid black, cut:

- 1—1½x12½" strip
- 18—2½" squares

1. Referring to Cut and Assemble the Sashing Units on *page 40,* Step 2, use a Pattern E foundation paper, the solid red 2½" squares, and nine solid black 2½" squares to make a sawtooth sashing strip. Repeat to make a second sawtooth sashing strip using a foundation paper, the solid blue 2½" squares, and the remaining solid black 2½" squares.

2. Referring to the photograph *opposite,* sew the two sawtooth sashing strips to the solid black 1½x12½" strip to make a sashing unit.

Cut and Assemble the Sashing Squares

From solid white, cut:

- 84—2⅞" squares, cutting each in half diagonally for a total of 168 triangles

From solid black, cut:

- 84—2⅞" squares, cutting each in half diagonally for a total of 168 triangles

1. Sew together one solid white triangle and one solid black triangle to make a triangle-square (see Diagram 20). Press the seam allowance toward the solid black triangle. The pieced triangle square should measure 2½" square, including the seam allowances. Repeat to make a total of 168 triangle-squares.

Diagram 20

2. Sew together four triangle-squares in pairs (see Diagram 21). Press the seam allowances in opposite directions. Then join the pairs to make a sashing square. The pieced sashing square should measure 4½" square, including the seam allowances. Repeat to make a total of 42 sashing squares.

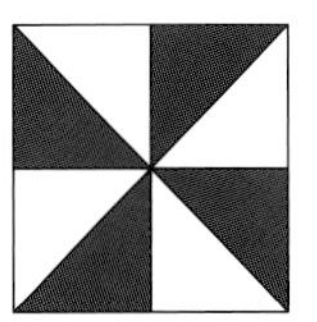

Diagram 21

Assemble the Quilt Top

1. Referring to the photograph *opposite,* lay out the race car print 12½" squares, the 71 sashing units, and the 42 sashing squares in 13 horizontal rows.

2. Sew together the pieces in each row. Press the seam allowances toward the blocks or the sashing squares. Then join the rows to complete the quilt top. Press the seam allowances in one direction.

Complete the Quilt

From black-and-white check, cut:

- 10—2½x42" binding strips

1. Layer the quilt top, batting, and backing according to the instructions in Quilter's Schoolhouse, which begins on *page 150.*

2. Quilt as desired. Quiltmaker April West used variegated thread to machine-quilt curvy lines that look like tire tread marks.

3. Use the black-and-white check 2½x42" strips to bind the quilt according to the instructions in Quilter's Schoolhouse.

TABLE TOPPER

Want to try your hand at foundation piecing? This project is the perfect sampler.

Materials

9×22" piece (fat eighth) of cream print for block

9×22" piece (fat eighth) of red stripe for block

1⅓ yards of blue print for block, sashing, binding, and backing

⅛ yard of light gold print for block

2—9×22" pieces (fat eighth) of assorted gray prints for block

½ yard of gold print for sashing

⅜ yard of red print for sashing

18×22" piece (fat quarter) of red plaid for sashing

26" square of quilt batting

Finished table topper: 20" square

Cut the Fabrics

To make the best use of your fabrics, cut the pieces in the order that follows. This project uses "Mississippi Wheel of Fortune" patterns, which are on *Pattern Sheet 2*. To make templates of the patterns, follow the instructions in Quilter's Schoolhouse, which begins on *page 150*.

Cut and Assemble the Block

From cream print, cut:
- 8 of Pattern A

From red stripe, cut:
- 8 of Pattern A

From blue print, cut:
- 16—2½×3" rectangles
- 1 of Pattern B

From light gold print, cut:
- 16—2½×3" rectangles

From gray print No. 1, cut:
- 4 of Pattern D

From gray print No. 2, cut:
- 4 of Pattern D reversed

1. Referring to Cut and Assemble the Wheel of Fortune Blocks on *page 38*, Step 1, use the cream print and red stripe A pieces to make a swirl circle.

2. Press under the blue print B circle seam allowance, center the B circle over the swirl circle, and machine-stitch the B circle in place.

3. Referring to Make the Foundation Papers on *page 39*, make a total of four perforated Pattern C foundation papers and eight Pattern E foundation papers.

4. Referring to Assemble the Sawtooth Circles on *page 39*, steps 1 through 6, use the blue print rectangles and light gold print rectangles to make a sawtooth circle.

5. Position the swirl circle atop the sawtooth circle opening. Join the circles.

6. Sew together the four gray print No. 1 D pieces and the four gray print No. 2 D pieces to make a square frame. Place the sawtooth circle on the square frame opening; join the pieces to make the block.

Cut and Assemble the Sashing Units

The cutting and piecing instructions that follow result in one sashing unit. Repeat to make a total of four sashing units.

From gold print, cut:
- 18—2½" squares

From red print, cut:
- 8—2½" squares

From blue print, cut:
- 8—2½" squares

From red plaid, cut:
- 1—1½×12½" strip

1. Referring to Cut and Assemble the Sashing Units on *page 40*, Step 2, use a Pattern E foundation paper, nine gold print 2½" squares, and the red print 2½" squares to make a sawtooth sashing strip. Repeat to make a second sawtooth sashing strip using a foundation paper, the blue print 2½" squares, and the remaining gold print 2½" squares.

2. Referring to the photograph *opposite*, sew the two sawtooth sashing strips to the red plaid 1½×12½" strip to make a sashing unit.

Cut and Assemble the Sashing Squares

The cutting and piecing instructions that follow are for one sashing square. Repeat to make a total of four sashing squares.

From red print, cut:
- 4 of Pattern F

From blue print, cut:
- 4 of Pattern G

Referring to Cut and Assemble the Sashing Squares on *page 42*, use the red print and blue print pieces to make a sashing square.

Assemble the Quilt Top

1. Referring to photograph *opposite* for placement, lay out the block, the four sashing units, and the four sashing squares in three horizontal rows.

2. Sew together the pieces in each row. Press the seam allowances toward the block or the sashing squares. Then join the rows to complete the quilt top. Press the seam allowances in one direction.

Complete the Quilt Top

From blue print, cut:
- 2—2½×42" binding strips

1. Layer the quilt top, batting, and backing according to instructions in Quilter's Schoolhouse, which begins on *page 150*. Quilt as desired.

2. Use the blue print 2½×42" strips to bind the quilt according to the instructions in Quilter's Schoolhouse.

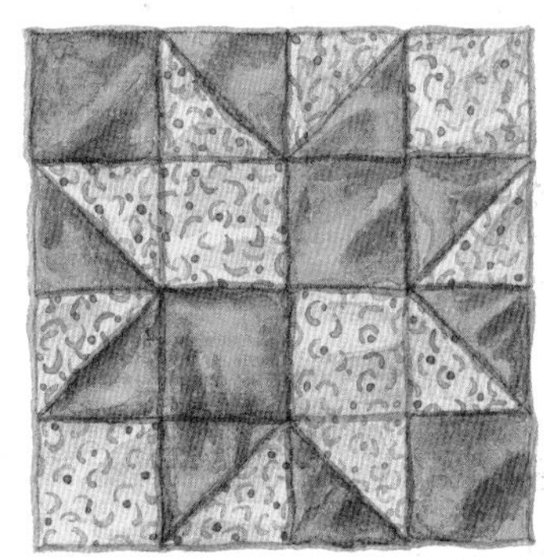

SUNRISE, *Sunset*

Designer Joy Hoffman combined cool purple, warm orange, and gold to give this quilt top depth and to illustrate opposite times of day: dawn and dusk. Her nontraditional sashing placement generates a sense of movement in the quilt.

Materials

2¼ yards of light gold print for blocks

2¼ yards total of assorted purple and orange prints for blocks

⅞ yard of multicolor stripe for sashing

¼ yard of bright orange print for inner border

2¼ yards of multicolor print for outer border

⅝ yard of purple print for binding

4 yards of backing fabric

70×80" of quilt batting

Finished quilt top: 64×73½"
Finished block: 8" square

Quantities specified for 44/45"-wide, 100% cotton fabrics. All measurements include a ¼" seam allowance. Sew with right sides together unless otherwise stated.

continued

Designer Notes

With this quilt, Joy Hoffman elevated the two-color block to a new level. She used a variety of purple and orange prints to give the blocks distinct personalities, but united them by combining the purple or orange pieces with the same light gold print. A rather funky stripe prompted the unusual sashing, which only appears complicated.

"Let the fabric speak to you," Joy says. "When I found that stripe, I thought, *Oh, this would be interesting.*"

To develop your own design, Joy encourages thinking outside the box. "Make some blocks and think how you'd like them to be arranged," she says. "It doesn't always have to be a traditional layout."

Cut the Fabrics

To make the best use of your fabrics, cut the pieces in the order that follows. Cut the outer border strips the length of the fabric (parallel to the selvage).

Before cutting, note that the designer grouped the assorted purple prints and orange prints into sets when cutting out the triangles and squares, so that each finished block was created from two fabrics.

From light gold print, cut:
- 168—2⅞" squares, cutting each in half diagonally for a total of 336 triangles
- 168—2½" squares

From assorted purple prints, cut:
- 84—2⅞" squares, cutting each in half diagonally for a total of 168 triangles (21 sets of 8 triangles
- 84—2½" squares (21 sets of 4 squares to match each triangle set *above*)

From assorted orange prints, cut:
- 84—2⅞" squares, cutting each in half diagonally for a total of 168 triangles (21 sets of 8 triangles
- 84—2½" squares (21 sets of 4 squares to match each triangle set *above*)

From multicolor stripe, cut:
- 13—2×42" strips for sashing

From bright orange print, cut:
- 6—1×42" strips for inner border

From multicolor print, cut:
- 2—5×74" outer border strips
- 2—5×55½" outer border strips

From purple print, cut:
- 7—2¼×42" binding strips

Assemble the Blocks

The following instructions are for making one purple block. Repeat the steps to make a total of 21 purple blocks and 21 orange blocks.

1. For one block you'll need one set of matching purple print pieces (eight triangles and four 2½" squares), eight light gold print triangles, and four light gold print 2½" squares.

2. Sew together one purple print triangle and one light gold print triangle to make a triangle-square (see Diagram 1). Press the seam allowance toward the purple triangle. The pieced triangle-square should measure 2½" square, including the seam allowances. Repeat to make a total of eight triangle-squares.

Diagram 1

3. Referring to Diagram 2 for placement, sew together two triangle-squares, one purple print 2½" square, and one light gold print 2½" square in pairs. Press the seam allowances toward the squares. Then join the pairs to make a unit A. Press the seam allowance open. Unit A should measure 4½" square, including the seam allowances. Repeat to make a second unit A.

Diagram 2

Diagram 3

4. Referring to Diagram 3, sew together two triangle-squares, one purple print 2½" square, and one light gold print 2½" square in pairs. Press the seam allowances toward the squares. Then join the pairs to make a unit B. Press the seam allowance open. Unit B should measure 4½" square, including the seam allowances. Repeat to make a second unit B.

5. Referring to Diagram 4, pair each unit A with a unit B; sew together each pair. Press the seam allowances in opposite directions. Then join the pairs to make a block. Press the seam allowance open. The pieced block should measure 8½" square, including the seam allowances.

Diagram 4

Assemble the Quilt Center

1. Cut and piece the multicolor stripe 2×42" strips to make the following:

- 2—2×64" sashing strips
- 4—2×51½" sashing strips
- 1—2×34" sashing strip
- 1—2×26" sashing strip
- 6—2×16½" sashing strips
- 1—2×8½" sashing strip

2. Referring to the Quilt Assembly Diagram and the photograph on *page 52*, lay out the blocks and the multicolor stripe sashing strips in the sections indicated. Sew together the blocks into groups

Quilt Assembly Diagram

continued

as shown; press open the seam allowances. Then join the block groups with sashing strips to make sections 1, 2, and 3. Press the seam allowances toward the sashing strips.

3. Sew together the three pieced sections. Press the seam allowances toward the sashing strips. Add the multicolor stripe 2×64" sashing strips to the long edges of the pieced sections to complete the quilt center. Press the seam allowances toward the sashing strips. The pieced quilt center should measure 54½×64", including the seam allowances.

Add the Borders

1. Cut and piece the bright orange print 1×42" strips to make the following:
   - 2—1×65" inner border strips
   - 2—1×54½" inner border strips

2. Add the short inner border strips to the short edges of the pieced quilt center. Then join the long inner border strips to the long edges of the pieced quilt center. Press all seam allowances toward the inner border.

3. Add the multicolor print 5×55½" outer border strips to the short edges of the pieced quilt center. Then join the multicolor print 5×74" outer border strips to the long edges of the pieced quilt center to complete the quilt top. Press all seam allowances toward the outer border.

Complete the Quilt

1. Layer the quilt top, batting, and backing according to the instructions in Quilter's Schoolhouse, which begins on *page 150*.

2. Quilt as desired. Joy machine-quilted free-form arcs and rays to emphasize the sunrise-sunset theme.

3. Use the purple print 2¼×42" strips to bind the quilt according to the instructions in Quilter's Schoolhouse.

optional colors

Quilt tester Laura Boehnke experimented with the placement of sashing strips in the colorful wall hanging *below left*. In the quilt *below*, Laura chose a diagonal stripe print for the outer border. This allowed her to cut the border strips on the straight of grain but still add visual interest to the finished quilt.

WALL ART

These framed pieces reflect subtle shifts in color evoke the beauty of the setting sun.

Materials

Scraps of assorted batiks in shades of yellow, orange, and red

Scraps of assorted batiks in shades of blue and purple

4—22" squares of muslin for lining

4—22" squares of quilt batting

Finished framed piece: 16" square

Cut the Fabrics

To make the best use of your fabrics, cut the pieces in the order that follows. Each unit is made of two predominant colors. In the grouping in the photograph *above*, the units move from blue-and-yellow units in the upper left-hand corner to red-and-purple units in the lower right-hand corner. Use a design wall to help you create a pleasing arrangement.

From assorted yellow, orange, and red batiks, cut:
- 64—2⅞" squares, cutting them in half diagonally for a total of 128 triangles (64 sets of 2 matching triangles)
- 64—2½" squares (1 square to match each set of triangles *above*)

From assorted blue and purple batiks, cut:
- 64—2⅞" squares, cutting them in half diagonally for a total of 128 triangles (64 sets of 2 matching triangles)
- 64—2½" squares (1 square to match each set of triangles *above*)

Assemble the Units

1. Referring to the photograph *opposite* for placement and Assemble the Blocks on *page 50*, steps 2 and 3, use one set of yellow, orange, or red batik pieces (two triangles and one 2½" square) and one set of blue or purple batik pieces (two triangles and one 2½" square) to make a unit A. Repeat to make a total of 32 of unit A.

2. Referring to Assemble the Blocks on *page 50*, steps 2 and 4, use one set of yellow, orange, or red batik pieces (two triangles and one 2½" square) and one set of blue or purple batik pieces (two triangles and one 2½" square) to make a unit B. Repeat to make a total of 32 of unit B.

Assemble the Block Sets

1. Referring to the photograph *opposite*, arrange the pieced units on a design wall in four groups of 16 units each.

2. Within each group, sew together the units in rows. Press the seam allowances open. Then join the rows to make four block sets. Press the seam allowances open. Each pieced block set should measure 16½" square, including seam allowances.

Complete the Quilts

1. Layer each block set with a 22" square of batting and a muslin 22" square according to the instructions in Quilter's Schoolhouse, which begins on *page 150*.

2. Quilt as desired. Mabeth Oxenreider machine-quilted a sun in the corner of the upper left-hand block. She then quilted the sun's rays across the four block sets.

3. Frame the block sets as desired.

THROW

Blue-and-white quilts have a clean and classic look.

continued

Materials

2⅝ yards of assorted white prints for blocks and outer border

2⅝ yards of assorted blue prints for blocks and outer border

1 yard of dark blue print for inner border and binding

3½ yards of backing fabric

62×70" of quilt batting

Finished quilt top: 56×64"

Cut the Fabrics

To make the best use of your fabrics, cut the pieces in the order that follows.

From assorted white prints, cut:

- 168—2⅞" squares, cutting each in half diagonally for a total of 336 triangles (42 sets of 8 matching triangles)
- 168—2½" squares (42 sets of 2 squares to match each triangle set *above*)
- 56—2⅞" squares, cutting each in half diagonally for a total of 112 triangles
- 4—2½" squares

From assorted blue prints, cut:

- 168—2⅞" squares, cutting each in half diagonally for a total of 336 triangles (42 sets of 8 matching triangles)
- 168—2½" squares (42 sets of 2 squares to match each triangle set *above*)
- 56—2⅞" squares, cutting each in half diagonally for a total of 112 triangles

From dark blue print, cut:

- 12—2½×42" strips for inner border and binding

Assemble the Blocks

Referring to the photograph *opposite* for placement and Assemble the Blocks on *page 50*, steps 2 through 5, use a set of matching white print pieces (eight triangles and four 2½" squares) and a set of matching blue print pieces (eight triangles and four 2½" squares) to make a block. Repeat to make a total of 42 blocks.

Assemble the Quilt Center

1. Referring to the photograph *opposite*, lay out the 42 pieced blocks in seven horizontal rows.

2. Sew together the blocks in each row. Press the seam allowances in one direction, alternating the direction with each row. Then join the rows to make the quilt center. Press the seam allowances in one direction. The pieced quilt center should measure 48½×56½", including seam allowances.

Assemble and Add the Borders

1. Cut and piece six of the dark blue print 2½×42" strips to make the following:
   - 2—2½×56½" inner border strips
   - 2—2½×52½" inner border strips

2. Sew the long dark blue print inner border strips to the long edges of the quilt center. Add the short dark blue print inner border strips to the short edges of the quilt center. Press all seam allowances toward the inner border.

3. Sew together one remaining white print triangle and one remaining blue print triangle to make a triangle-square (see Diagram 5). Press the seam allowance toward the blue print triangle. The pieced triangle square should measure 2½" square, including the seam allowance. Repeat to make a total of 112 triangle-squares.

Diagram 5

4. Referring to the photograph *opposite* for placement, sew together 30 triangle-squares to make a long outer border strip. The pieced long outer border strip should measure 2½×60½", including the seam allowances. Repeat to make a second pieced long outer border strip.

5. Referring to the photograph *opposite*, sew together 26 triangle-squares and two white print 2½" squares to make a short outer border strip. The pieced short outer border strip should measure 2½×56½", including the seam allowances. Repeat to make a second pieced short outer border strip.

6. Sew the pieced long outer border strips to the long edges of the quilt center. Add the pieced short outer border strips to the short edges of the

quilt center to complete the quilt top. Press the seam allowances toward the inner border.

Complete the Quilt

1. Layer the quilt top, batting, and backing according to the instructions in Quilter's Schoolhouse, which begins on *page 150*.
2. Quilt as desired. Machine-quilter April West stitched a swirl pattern over the entire quilt.
3. Use the remaining dark blue print 2½×42" strips to bind the quilt according to the instructions in Quilter's Schoolhouse.

Bali *Ho*

Black sateen sets off a wave of brilliant color in designer Betty Alvarez's contemporary twist on the traditional Old Maid's Puzzle. Using light prints in the small triangle-squares creates a star-in-a-star effect.

Materials

6⅞ yards of black sateen for blocks and binding
60—5×10" pieces of assorted dark prints in blue, purple, green, and gold for blocks
60—6" squares of assorted light, bright prints in yellow, orange, red, and green for blocks
7¼ yards of backing fabric
86×102" of quilt batting

Finished quilt top: 80×96"
Finished block: 16" square

Quantities specified for 44/45"-wide, 100% cotton fabrics. All measurements include a ¼" seam allowance. Sew with right sides together unless otherwise stated.

Designer Notes

The catalyst for this quilt was Betty Alvarez's desire to play with color. To make it work, she gave each of nine quilting friends a fat quarter of the black background fabric and asked for two blocks using the range of colors given in the materials list.

"My goal was progression of color. I wanted the large stars to be the blues and greens, and the small stars to be the yellows through the oranges. And I knew I wanted a sparkle in the middle," Betty says of her "Bali Ho" quilt.

"Because I had made that decision, and because of how I received the blocks, I could progress from one color to another pretty easily. Scrappy is a nice way to do this quilt. To me, to use different fabrics is great. I love that."

continued

Cut the Fabrics

To make the best use of your fabrics, cut the pieces in the order that follows.

From black sateen, cut:

- 9—2½×42" binding strips
- 120—4⅞" squares
- 240—2⅞" squares
- 480—2½" squares

From *each* assorted dark print, cut:

- 2—4⅞" squares

From *each* assorted light print, cut:

- 4—2⅞" squares

Assemble the Quilt Top

1. Use a quilter's pencil to mark a diagonal line on the wrong side of the black sateen 4⅞" squares and the black sateen 2⅞" squares. (To prevent the fabric from stretching as you draw the lines, place 220-grit sandpaper under the squares.)

2. Layer each marked black sateen 4⅞" square atop an assorted dark print 4⅞" square. Sew each pair together with two seams, stitching ¼" on each side of the drawn line (see Diagram 1).

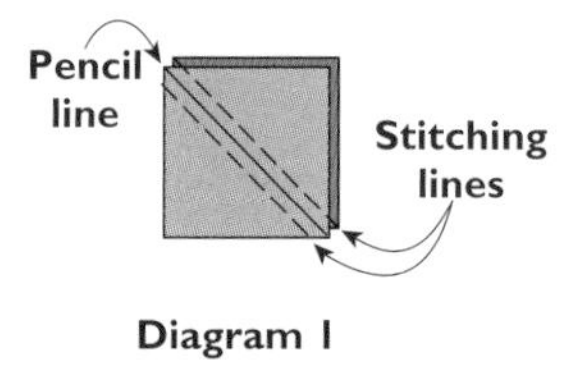

Diagram 1

3. Cut a pair apart on the drawn line to make two triangle units (see Diagram 2). Press the triangle units open to make two large triangle-squares

(see Diagram 3). Each large triangle-square should measure 4½" square, including the seam allowances. Repeat to make a total of 240 large triangle-squares.

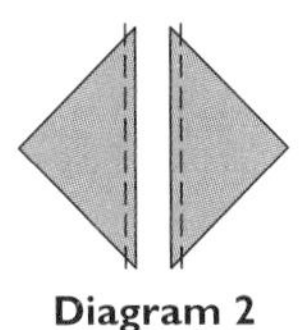

Diagram 2

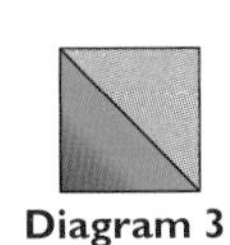

Diagram 3

4. Repeat steps 2 and 3 using the marked black sateen 2⅞" squares and the assorted light print 2⅞" squares to make 480 small triangle-squares (see Diagram 4). Each small triangle-square should measure 2½" square, including the seam allowances.

Diagram 4

5. Using the photograph *opposite* for placement ideas, lay out the small and large triangle-squares and the black sateen 2½" squares in blocks (see Diagram 5). Betty used a design wall, moving the pieces until she was pleased with each block combination. "I just sat back and watched [the wall] for a few days," Betty says. "I replaced one for another until it was just right."

6. When you are pleased with your arrangement, sew together the pieces in one block, first joining them in four horizontal rows (see Diagram 5). Press the seam allowances in one direction, alternating the direction with each row. Then join the rows to make a block. Press the seam allowances in one direction. The pieced block should measure 16½" square, including the seam allowances. Return the block to its position in the layout and repeat to make a total of 30 blocks.

Diagram 5

7. Sew together the blocks in each row. Press the seam allowances in one direction, alternating the direction with the row. Then join the rows to complete the quilt top. Press the seam allowances in one direction.

Complete the Quilt

1. Layer the quilt top, batting, and backing according to the instructions in Quilter's Schoolhouse, which begins on *page 150*. Quilt as desired.

2. Use the black sateen 2½×42" strips to bind the quilt according to the instructions in Quilter's Schoolhouse.

optional colors

Rather than duplicating the rainbow effect of the original color palette, quilt tester Laura Boehnke made nine big star blocks using a blue print for the points and light prints for the backgrounds.

"For the smaller star points, I chose red prints," Laura says. "I controlled it so that each star has the same print. For the corners, I made orange points."

FLOOR PILLOW

One large star block makes a pillow ample enough to use for casual seating.

Materials

2 yards of brown print for block, inner border, and pillow back

⅛ yard of beige print for block

⅝ yard of gold print for block and outer border

⅛ yard of green print for block

30" square of muslin for lining

30" square of quilt batting

24"-square pillow form

Finished pillow: 24" square

Cut the Fabrics

To make the best use of your fabrics, cut the pieces in the order that follows.

From brown print, cut:

- 2—24½x30" rectangles
- 2—2x19½" inner border strips
- 2—2x16½" inner border strips
- 4—4⅞" squares
- 8—2⅞" squares
- 16—2½" squares

From beige print, cut:

- 4—2⅞" squares

From gold print, cut:

- 2—3x24½" outer border strips
- 2—3x19½" outer border strips
- 4—4⅞" squares

From green print, cut:

- 4—2⅞" squares

Assemble the Pillow Center

1. Referring to Assemble the Quilt Top on *page 60*, steps 1 through 3, use the four brown print 4⅞" squares and four gold print 4⅞" squares to make a total of eight brown-and-gold large triangle-squares.

2. In the same manner, use four brown print 2⅞" squares and four beige print 2⅞" squares to make a total of eight brown-and-beige small triangle-squares. Use four brown print 2⅞" squares and four green print 2⅞" squares to make a total of eight brown-and-green small triangle-squares.

3. Using the photograph *above left* for placement, lay out the small and large triangle-squares and the brown print 2½" squares in rows. Sew together the pieces in the rows. Press the seam allowances in one direction, alternating the direction with each row. Then join the rows to make a block. The pieced block should measure 16½" square, including the seam allowances.

Add the Borders

1. Sew the brown print 2x16½" inner border strips to opposite edges of the block. Add the brown print 2x19½" inner border strips to the remaining edges of the block. Press all the seam allowances toward the inner border.

2. Sew the gold print 3x19½" outer border strips to opposite edges of the block. Add the gold print 3x24½" outer border strips to the remaining edges of the block to complete the pillow top. Press the seam allowances toward the outer border.

Complete the Pillow

1. Layer the pillow top, batting, and muslin lining according to instructions in Quilter's Schoolhouse, which begins on *page 150*. Quilt as desired. Trim the batting and lining even with the pillow top edges.

2. With wrong sides inside, fold each brown print 24½×30" rectangle in half to form two double-thick 15×24½" pieces. Overlap the folded edges by 6". Stitch ¼" from the top and bottom edges, including across the folds, to secure the pieces, and create the pillow back.

3. With right sides together, layer the pillow top and the pillow back. Sew together the pieces along all four edges; turn right side out. Insert the pillow form through the back opening.

THROW

Pieced sashing and border strips showcase each block and continue the star motif.

Materials

⅝ yard of red print No. 1 for blocks

⅝ yard of red print No. 2 for blocks

⅞ yard of beige print for blocks

⅝ yard of green print for blocks

⅞ yard of red print No. 3 for sashing and border

2½ yards of brown stripe for sashing and border

3 yards of backing fabric

54×74" of quilt batting

Finished quilt top: 48×68"

Cut the Fabrics

To make the best use of your fabrics, cut the pieces in the order that follows.

From red print No. 1, cut:
- 48—2⅞" squares
- 24—2½" squares

From red print No. 2, cut:
- 24—4⅞" squares

From beige print, cut:
- 48—2⅞" squares
- 72—2½" squares

From green print, cut:
- 24—4⅞" squares

From red print No. 3, cut:
- 12—4½" squares
- 96—2½" squares

From brown stripe, cut:
- 6—2½×42" binding strips
- 17—4½×16½" rectangles
- 10—2½×16½" rectangles
- 14—2½×4½" rectangles
- 4—2½" squares

continued

Assemble the Blocks

1. Referring to Assemble the Quilt Top on *page 60*, steps 1 through 3, use the 24 red print No. 2-4⅞" squares and the 24 green print 4⅞" squares to make a total of 48 large triangle-squares.

2. In the same manner, use the 48 red print No. 1-2⅞" squares and the 48 beige print 2⅞" squares to make a total of 96 small triangle-squares.

3. Using the photograph *opposite* for placement, lay out eight each of the small and large triangle-squares, four red print No. 1-2½" squares, and 12 beige print 2½" squares in rows. Sew together the pieces in each row. Press the seam allowances toward the large triangle-squares. Then join the rows to make a block. Press the seam allowances in one direction. The pieced block should measure 16½" square, including the seam allowances. Repeat to make a total of six blocks.

Assemble the Quilt Center

1. Use a quilter's pencil to mark a diagonal line on the wrong side of 96 red print No. 3-2½" squares; set aside 28 marked squares.

2. Align a marked red print No. 3-2½" square with one corner of a brown stripe 4½×16½" rectangle (see Diagram 6; note the placement of the marked diagonal line). Stitch on the marked line; trim away the excess fabric, leaving a ¼" seam allowance. Press the attached triangle open.

Diagram 6

3. Repeat Step 2 in the remaining corners of the brown stripe rectangle to make a sashing unit. The pieced sashing unit should still measure 4½×16½", including the seam allowances.

4. Repeat steps 2 and 3 to make a total of 17 sashing units.

5. Referring to the photograph *opposite*, lay out the six blocks, the 12 red print No. 3-4½" squares, and the 17 sashing units. Sew together the pieces in each row. Press the seam allowances toward the sashing units. Then join the rows to make the quilt center. The pieced quilt center should measure 44½×64½", including the seam allowances.

Assemble and Add the Border

1. Align a reserved marked red print 2½" square with one end of a brown stripe 2½×4½" rectangle (see Diagram 7; note the placement of the marked diagonal line). Stitch on the marked line; trim away the excess fabric, leaving a ¼" seam allowance. Press the attached triangle open.

Diagram 7

2. In the same manner, align a second marked red print 2½" square with the opposite end of the brown stripe 2½×4½" rectangle (see Diagram 7, again noting the placement of the marked line). Stitch on the marked line; trim and press as before to make a Flying Geese unit. The pieced Flying Geese unit should still measure 2½×4½", including the seam allowances.

3. Repeat steps 1 and 2 to make a total of 14 Flying Geese units.

4. Referring to the photograph *opposite*, lay out four Flying Geese units and three brown stripe 2½×16½" rectangles. Sew the pieces together to make a long border unit. Press the seam allowances toward the brown stripe rectangles. The pieced long border unit should measure 2½×64½", including the seam allowances. Repeat to make a second long border unit.

5. Referring to the photograph *opposite*, lay out two brown stripe 2½" squares, three Flying Geese units, and two brown stripe 2½×16½" rectangles. Sew the pieces together to make a pieced short border unit; press the seam allowances toward the brown stripe rectangles. The pieced short border unit should measure 2½×48½", including the seam allowances. Repeat to make a second pieced short border unit.

6. Sew the long border units to the long edges of the pieced quilt center. Sew the short border units to the short edges of the pieced quilt center to complete the quilt top. Press all seam allowances toward the border.

Complete the Quilt

1. Layer the quilt top, batting, and backing according to the instructions in Quilter's Schoolhouse, which begins on *page 150*. Quilt as desired.
2. Use the brown stripe 2½×42" strips to bind the quilt according to the instructions in Quilter's Schoolhouse.

ROTARY MAGIC

Zip through the preparation process with completely rotary-cut quilts. "Flickering Stars" with its heirloom-style appeal, dashing "Dolly Madison," and scrappy "Sunshine and Shade" offer the opportunity to explore a few of the many patterns created with triangles and squares. New projects show you how to extract elements of a favorite quilt to form a different rotary-cut design.

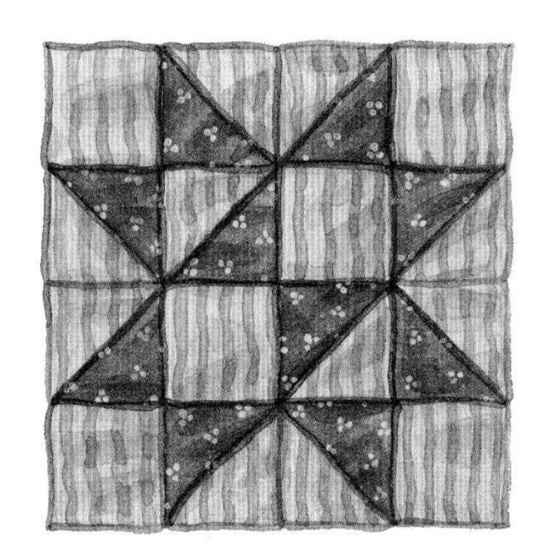

FLICKERING *Stars*

Stars, a long-time favorite motif, continue to be popular today. Quilt designers Andria and Sarah Grant created this field of stars using quick cutting and piecing techniques to achieve an heirloom look.

Materials

1¾ yards total of assorted red, blue, and gold prints for blocks and inner sashing
2½ yards total of assorted light prints for blocks and inner sashing
¾ yard of light tan print for outer sashing
1¾ yards of blue print for border
⅞ yard of red print for binding
3½ yards of backing fabric
61×76" of quilt batting

Finished quilt top: 54½×69"
Finished block: 6" square

Quantities specified for 44/45"-wide, 100% cotton fabrics. All measurements include a ¼" seam allowance. Sew with right sides together unless otherwise stated.

Cut the Fabrics

To make the best use of your fabrics, cut the pieces in the order that follows. Cut the border strips lengthwise (parallel to the selvage).

Before cutting, note that the designers grouped the assorted red, blue, gold, and light prints into sets when cutting out the triangles and 2" squares, so that each finished star was created from two fabrics.

continued

From assorted red, blue, and gold prints, cut:

- 175—2⅜" squares, cutting each in half diagonally for a total of 350 triangles (35 sets of 10 matching triangles)
- 48—1¾" squares for sashing stars (1 to match each set of matching 1¼" squares *below*)
- 384—1¼" squares (48 sets of 8 matching squares) for sashing stars

From assorted light prints, cut:

- 175—2⅜" squares, cutting each in half diagonally for a total of 350 triangles (35 sets of 10 matching triangles)
- 210—2" squares (35 sets of 6 matching squares)
- 82—1¾x6½" rectangles

From light tan print, cut:

- 24—3x6½" rectangles
- 4—3" squares
- 28—1¾x3" rectangles

From blue print, cut:

- 2—6½x57½" border strips
- 2—6½x55" border strips

From red print, cut:

- 7—2½x42" binding strips

Assemble the Star Blocks

The following piecing instructions use a red print fabric set and result in one star block. Repeat these steps with the red, blue, and gold print triangles to make a total of 35 star blocks.

1. For one block you'll need one set of 10 red print triangles, one set of 10 light print triangles, and six light print squares.

2. Sew together one red print triangle and one light print triangle to make a triangle-square (see Diagram 1). Press the seam allowance toward the red print triangle. The pieced triangle-square should measure 2" square, including the seam allowances. Repeat to make a total of 10 triangle-squares.

Diagram 1

3. Referring to Diagram 2 for placement, lay out the 10 triangle-squares and six light print 2" squares in four horizontal rows. Sew together the pieces in each row. Press the seam allowances in one direction, alternating the direction with each row. Join the rows to make a star block. Press the seam allowances in one direction. The pieced star block should measure 6½" square, including the seam allowances.

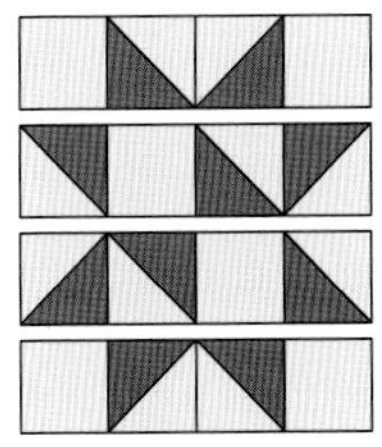

Diagram 2

Assemble the Sashing Strips

1. For accurate sewing lines, use a quilter's pencil to mark a diagonal line on the wrong side of the assorted red, blue, and gold print 1¼" squares. (To prevent your fabric from stretching as you draw the lines, place 220-grit sandpaper under the squares.)

2. Align a marked blue print 1¼" square with one corner of a light print 1¾x6½" rectangle (see Diagram 3; note the placement of the marked sewing line). Stitch on the marked line; trim away the excess fabric, leaving a ¼" seam allowance. Press the attached triangle open.

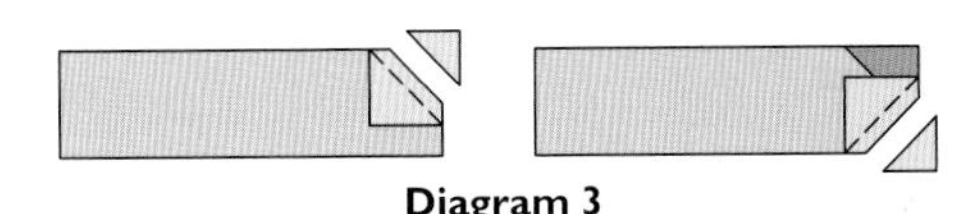

Diagram 3

3. In the same manner, add a second blue print 1¼" square to the adjacent corner of the same light print rectangle.

4. Repeat steps 2 and 3 using two marked red print 1¼" squares and the opposite corners of the same light print rectangle to make a pieced inner sashing strip (see Diagram 4). The pieced inner sashing strip should still measure 1¾x6½", including the seam allowances.

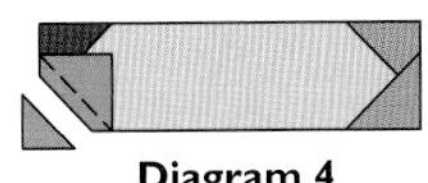

Diagram 4

5. Referring to the photograph *opposite* for color placement, repeat steps 2 through 4 using marked red, blue, and gold print 1¼" squares and the remaining light print 1¾x6½" rectangles to make a total of 82 inner sashing strips.

continued

Quilt Assembly Diagram

Note: To organize the piecing process, quilt tester Laura Boehnke suggests laying out the pieced star blocks and the pieces for the sashing strips on the floor or a design wall. Once you have the color placement correct, piece the sashing strips in order across each row.

6. Repeat steps 2 and 3 using the remaining marked red, blue, and gold print 1¼" squares and the 28 light tan print 1¾×3" rectangles to make a total of 28 outer sashing strips (see Diagram 5).

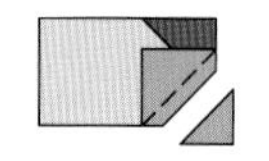
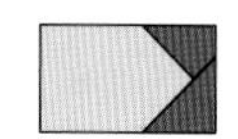

Diagram 5

Assemble the Quilt Center

1. Referring to the Quilt Assembly Diagram and the photograph on *page 70*, lay out the 35 star blocks; the 82 pieced inner sashing strips; the 48 assorted red, blue, and gold print 1¾" sashing squares; the 28 pieced outer sashing strips; the 24 light tan print 3×6½" outer sashing rectangles; and the four light tan print 3" outer sashing squares in 17 horizontal rows. Make sure each of the stars formed by the pieced sashing strips, 1¾" sashing squares, and pieced outer sashing strips are composed of one color.

2. Sew together the pieces in each row. Press the seam allowances in one direction, alternating the direction with each row. Join the rows to make the quilt center. Press the seam allowances in one direction. The pieced quilt center should measure 43×57½", including the seam allowances.

Add the Border

1. Sew the blue print 6½×57½" border strips to the long edges of the pieced quilt center. Press the seam allowances toward the blue print border.

2. Add the blue print 6½×55" border strips to the short edges of the pieced quilt center to complete the quilt top. Press the seam allowances toward the blue print border.

Complete the Quilt

1. Layer the quilt top, batting, and backing according to the instructions in Quilter's Schoolhouse, which begins on *page 150*.

2. Quilt as desired. An allover meandering design was quilted on the featured quilt. Tan thread was used in the quilt center, and blue thread was used in the border.

3. Use the red print 2½×42" strips to bind the quilt according to the instructions in Quilter's Schoolhouse.

Flickering Stars Quilt

optional sizes

If you'd like to make this quilt in a size other than for a lap quilt, use the information *below*. The blue print yardage requirements are for cutting border strips across the fabric width, instead of parallel to the selvage.

Alternate quilt sizes	Crib/Wall	Full/Queen	King
Number of blocks	20	99	144
Number of inner sashing strips	49	218	312
Number of outer sashing strips	22	44	52
Number of blocks wide by long	4×5	9×11	12×12
Finished size	47¼×54½"	83½×98"	105¼" square
Yardage requirements			
Assorted red, blue, and gold prints	1¼ yards total	4 yards total	5½ yards total
Assorted light prints	1⅞ yards total	6 yards total	8⅓ yards total
Light tan print	⅝ yard	1 yard	1¼ yards
Blue print	1⅛ yards	2 yards	2⅜ yards
Red print	½ yard	⅞ yard	⅞ yard
Backing	3 yards	7½ yards	9⅓ yards
Batting	54×61"	90×104"	112" square

optional colors

Stars twinkle brighter than ever on quilt tester Laura Boehnke's version. Her choice of assorted bright prints, solids, and batiks makes a colorful statement quite different from the original quilt.

BED QUILT

Bold border fabric inspired the quilting design and the color of the setting squares.

Materials

2⅛ yards total of assorted red, blue, pink, and green prints for blocks

3¼ yards total of assorted cream prints for blocks

2⅔ yards of peach print for setting squares

¾ yard of green print for inner border

3¾ yards of brown floral for outer border and binding

7¾ yards of backing fabric

93×105" of quilt batting

Finished quilt top: 86½×98½"

Cut the Fabrics

To make the best use of your fabrics, cut the pieces in the order that follows. Cut the outer border strips lengthwise (parallel to the selvage).

Before cutting, note that the designer grouped the assorted red, blue, pink, green, and cream prints into sets when cutting out the triangles and 2" squares so that each finished star was created from two fabrics.

From assorted red, blue, pink, and green prints, cut:
- 360—2⅜" squares, cutting each in half diagonally for a total of 720 triangles (72 sets of 5 triangles)

From assorted cream prints, cut:
- 360—2⅜" squares, cutting each in half diagonally for a total of 720 triangles (72 sets of 5 triangles)
- 432—2" squares (72 sets of 6 squares to match each of the sets *above*)

From peach print, cut:
- 71—6½" squares

From green print, cut:
- 8—2½×42" strips for inner border

From brown floral, cut:
- 10—2½×42" binding strips
- 2—8¾×99" outer border strips
- 2—8¾×70½" outer border strips

Assemble the Star Blocks

Referring to the photograph *opposite* and Assemble the Star Blocks on *page 70*, use the assorted red, blue, pink, green, and cream print pieces to make 72 star blocks.

Assemble the Quilt Center

1. Referring to the photograph *opposite*, lay out the 72 star blocks and the 71 peach print 6½" squares in 13 horizontal rows.

2. Sew together the pieces in each row. Press the seam allowances in one direction, alternating the direction with each row. Join the rows to make the quilt center. Press the seam allowances in one direction. The pieced quilt center should measure 66½×78½", including the seam allowances.

Add the Borders

1. Cut and piece the green print 2½×42" strips to make the following:
   - 2—2½×82½" inner border strips
   - 2—2½×66½" inner border strips

2. Add the short green print inner border strips to the short edges of the pieced quilt center. Sew the long green print inner border strips to the long edges of the pieced quilt center. Press the seam allowances toward the green print inner border.

3. Sew the brown floral 8¾×70½" outer border strips to the short edges of the pieced quilt center. Sew the brown floral 8¾×99" outer border strips to the long edges of the pieced quilt center to complete the quilt top. Press the seam allowances toward the outer border.

Complete the Quilt

1. Layer the quilt top, batting, and backing according to the instructions in Quilter's Schoolhouse, which begins on *page 150*.

2. Quilt as desired. Sue Urich machine-quilted in the ditch in the star blocks and machine-quilted leaves in the peach print setting squares. In the green print inner border Sue machine-quilted wave shapes; in the outer border she quilted around the edges of the leaf and flower shapes.

3. Use the brown floral 2½×42" strips to bind the quilt according to the instructions in Quilter's Schoolhouse.

DOLLY MADISON'S *Star*

According to Barbara Brackman's Encyclopedia of Pieced Quilt Patterns, *this traditional block is also known as Santa Fe and President's Block. No matter what you call it, it's sure to land on your list of favorites once you've pieced it into a charming bed-size quilt.*

Materials

2⅞ yards of solid yellow for blocks and binding

5¼ yards of muslin for blocks

4⅔ yards of backing fabric

84" square of quilt batting

Finished quilt top: 78" square
Finished block: 18" square

Quantities specified for 44/45"-wide, 100% cotton fabrics. All measurements include a ¼" seam allowance. Sew with right sides together unless otherwise stated.

Cut the Fabrics

To make the best use of your fabrics, cut the pieces in the order that follows. Cut the sashing strips the length of the fabric (parallel to the selvage).

continued

From solid yellow, cut:
- 224—3" squares, cutting each in half diagonally for a total of 448 small triangles
- 5—2½×42" strips
- 8—2½×42" binding strips

From muslin, cut:
- 3—2½×78½" sashing strips
- 4—2½×42" strips
- 12—2½×18½" sashing strips
- 64—6½" squares
- 32—5⅛" squares, cutting each in half diagonally for a total of 64 large triangles
- 160—3" squares, cutting each in half diagonally for a total of 320 small triangles

Assemble the Nine-Patch Units

1. Aligning long edges, sew two solid yellow 2½×42" strips to a muslin 2½×42" strip to make a strip set A (see Diagram 1). Press the seam allowances toward the solid yellow strips. Repeat to make a second strip set A. Cut the strip sets into thirty-two 2½"-wide segments.

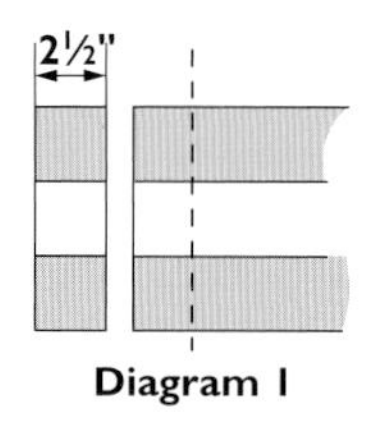

Diagram 1

2. Aligning long edges, sew two muslin 2½×42" strips to a solid yellow 2½×42" strip to make a strip set B (see Diagram 2). Press the seam allowances toward the solid yellow strip. Cut the strip set into sixteen 2½"-wide segments.

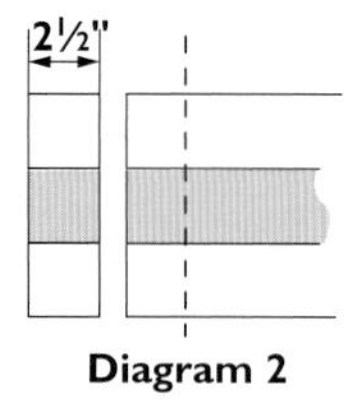

Diagram 2

3. Sew together two strip set A segments and one strip set B segment to make a Nine-Patch unit (see Diagram 3). Press the seam allowances toward the center segment. The Nine-Patch unit should measure 6½" square, including the seam allowances. Repeat to make a total of 16 Nine-Patch units.

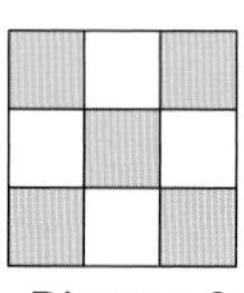
Diagram 3

Assemble the Star Point Units

1. Join one solid yellow small triangle and one muslin small triangle to make a triangle-square (see Diagram 4). Press the seam allowance toward the solid yellow triangle. The pieced triangle-square should measure 2⅝" square, including the seam allowances. Repeat to make a total of 192 triangle-squares.

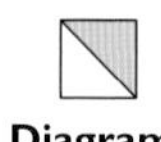
Diagram 4

2. Referring to Diagram 5 for placement, lay out a triangle-square and two muslin small triangles. Join the pieces to make a triangle unit 1. Press the seam allowances toward the triangle-square. Repeat to make a total of 64 of triangle unit 1.

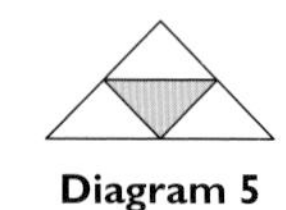
Diagram 5

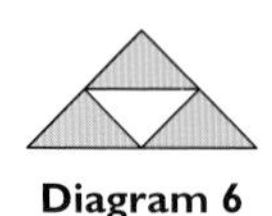
Diagram 6

3. Referring to Diagram 6, lay out a triangle-square and two solid yellow small triangles. Join the pieces to make a triangle unit 2. Press the seam allowances toward the solid yellow triangles. Repeat to make a total of 128 of triangle unit 2.

4. Referring to Diagram 7, lay out one triangle unit 1, two of triangle unit 2, and a muslin large triangle. Sew together the pieces in pairs. Press the seam allowances in opposite directions. Then join the pairs to make a star point unit. Press the seam allowances in one direction. The pieced star point unit should measure 6½" square, including the seam allowances. Repeat to make a total of 64 star point units.

Diagram 7

Assemble the Dolly Madison's Star Blocks

1. Referring to Diagram 8, lay out four star point units, four muslin 6½" squares, and one Nine-Patch unit in three horizontal rows.

2. Sew together the pieces in each row. Press the seam allowances toward the muslin squares or Nine-Patch unit. Then join the rows to make a Dolly Madison's Star block. Press the seam allowances in one direction. The pieced block should measure 18½" square, including the seam allowances.

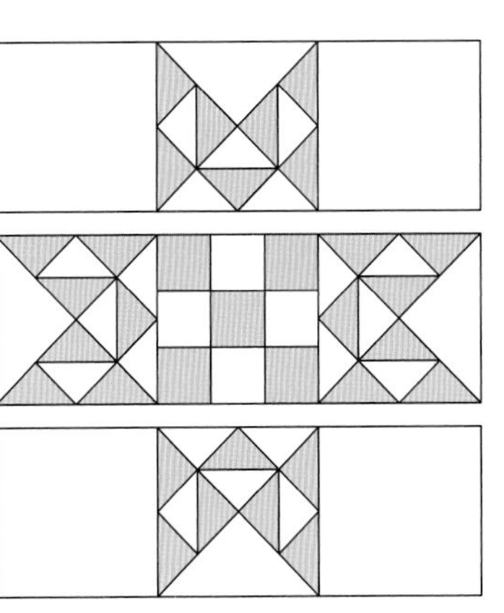

Diagram 8

continued

3. Repeat steps 1 and 2 to make a total of 16 Dolly Madison's Star blocks.

Assemble the Quilt Top

1. Referring to the photograph on *page 79*, lay out the 16 Dolly Madison's Star blocks and the 12 muslin 2½×18½" sashing strips in four horizontal rows. Sew together the blocks and sashing strips in each row. Press the seam allowances toward the sashing strips.

2. Lay out the pieced rows and the muslin 2½×78½" sashing strips; join to complete the quilt top. Press the seam allowances toward the sashing strips.

Complete the Quilt

1. Layer the quilt top, batting, and backing according to the instructions in Quilter's Schoolhouse, which begins on *page 150*.

2. Quilt as desired. This antique quilt was hand-quilted in a 1"-diagonal grid that changes direction several times within the quilt.

3. Use the solid yellow 2½×42" strips to bind the quilt according to the instructions in Quilter's Schoolhouse.

optional colors

Quilt tester Laura Boehnke chose a combination of solid fabrics to give her finished wall hanging an Amish look. The touch of yellow adds contrast to the deep blue-and-black color palette.

Dolly Madison's Star Quilt

optional sizes

If you'd like to make this quilt in a size other than for a twin bed, use the information *below*.

Alternate quilt sizes	Crib/Lap	Full	Queen/King
Number of blocks	9	20	25
Number of blocks wide by long	3×3	4×5	5×5
Finished size	58" square	78×98"	98"
Yardage requirements			
Solid yellow	2 yards	3⅓ yards	4 yards
Muslin	4 yards	6⅜ yards	8¼ yards
Backing	3½ yards	5⅞ yards	8⅔ yards
Batting	64" square	84×104"	104" square

SCRAPPY THROW

As this throw illustrates, repeating sections of large blocks offers alternate design possibilities.

Materials

2¾ yards total of assorted dark prints for blocks and binding

3⅝ yards of beige print for blocks and border

3⅝ yards of backing fabric

65×77" of quilt batting

Finished quilt top: 59×71"

Cut the Fabrics

To make the best use of your fabrics, cut the pieces in the order that follows.

From assorted dark prints, cut:

- 297—3" squares, cutting each in half diagonally for a total of 594 small triangles
- Enough 2½"-wide pieces in lengths varying from 8" to 11" to total 270" in length for binding

continued

From beige print, cut:
- 99—5⅛" squares, cutting each in half diagonally for a total of 198 large triangles
- 99—3" squares, cutting each in half diagonally for a total of 198 small triangles
- 7—3×42" strips for border

Assemble the Star Blocks

1. Referring to the photograph *opposite* and Assemble the Star Point Units on *page 78*, Step 1 and Step 3, use one beige print small triangle and three dark print small triangles to make a triangle unit 2. Repeat to make a total of 198 of triangle unit 2.

2. Sew together two triangle units and two beige print large triangles in pairs. Press the seam allowances in opposite directions. Then join the pairs to make a total of 99 star blocks.

Assemble the Quilt Top

1. Referring to the photograph *opposite* for placement, lay out the 99 star blocks in 11 horizontal rows.

2. Sew together the blocks in each row. Press the seam allowances in one direction, alternating the direction with each row. Join the rows to complete the quilt center. Press the seam allowances in one direction. The pieced quilt center should measure 54½×66½", including the seam allowances.

Add the Border

1. Cut and piece the beige print 3×42" strips to make the following:
- 2—3×71½" border strips
- 2—3×54½" border strips

2. Sew the short border strips to the short edges of the pieced quilt center. Add the long border strips to the long edges of the pieced quilt center to complete the quilt top. Press all the seam allowances toward the border.

Complete the Quilt

1. Layer the quilt top, batting, and backing according to the instructions in Quilter's Schoolhouse, which begins on *page 150*. Quilt as desired.

2. Piece the assorted dark print 2½"-wide pieces into a 270"-long strip. Use the pieced strip to bind the quilt according to the instructions in Quilter's Schoolhouse.

WALL HANGING

Color unifies the riot of prints contained within the blocks and the border.

Materials

2⅞ yards total of assorted bright prints for blocks and border

2 yards of assorted white prints for blocks

⅝ yard of black dot for binding

3⅔ yards of backing fabric

66" square of quilt batting

Finished quilt top: 60" square

continued

Cut the Fabrics

To make the best use of your fabrics, cut the pieces in the order that follows.

From assorted bright prints, cut:

- 12—3½x18½" rectangles for border
- 4—3½" squares for border corners
- 216—3" squares, cutting each in half diagonally for a total of 432 small triangles
- 81—2½" squares

From assorted white prints, cut:

- 36—6½" squares
- 18—5⅛" squares, cutting each in half diagonally for a total of 36 large triangles

From black dot, cut:

- 7—2½x42" binding strips

Assemble the Nine-Patch Units

Referring to the photograph *opposite*, use nine bright print 2½" squares to make a Nine-Patch unit (see Diagram 3 on *page 78*). Repeat to make a total of nine Nine-Patch units.

Assemble the Star Point Units

Referring to the photograph *opposite* and Assemble the Star Point Units on *page 78*, use 12 bright print small triangles and one white print large triangle to make a star point unit. Repeat to make a total of 36 star point units.

Assemble the Dolly Madison's Star Blocks

Referring to the photograph *opposite* and Assemble the Dolly Madison's Star Blocks on *page 79*, steps 1 and 2, use four star point units, four white print 6½" squares, and one Nine-Patch unit to make a Dolly Madison's Star block. Repeat to make a total of nine Dolly Madison's Star blocks.

Assemble the Quilt Center

1. Referring to the photograph *opposite* for placement, lay out the nine star blocks in three horizontal rows. Sew together the blocks in each row. Press the seam allowances in one direction, alternating the direction with each row.

2. Join the rows to complete the quilt center. Press the seam allowances in one direction. The pieced quilt center should measure 54½" square, including the seam allowances.

Add the Border

1. Piece the bright print 3½x18½" rectangles to make the following:
   - 4—3½x54½" border strips

2. Sew pieced border strips to opposite edges of the pieced quilt center. Sew bright print 3½" squares to both ends of the remaining pieced border strips. Add the pieced border strips to the remaining edges of the pieced quilt center to complete the quilt top. Press all seam allowances toward the border.

Complete the Quilt

1. Layer the quilt top, batting, and backing according to instructions in Quilter's Schoolhouse, which begins on *page 150*. Quilt as desired.

2. Use the black dot 2½x42" strips to bind the quilt according to the instructions in Quilter's Schoolhouse.

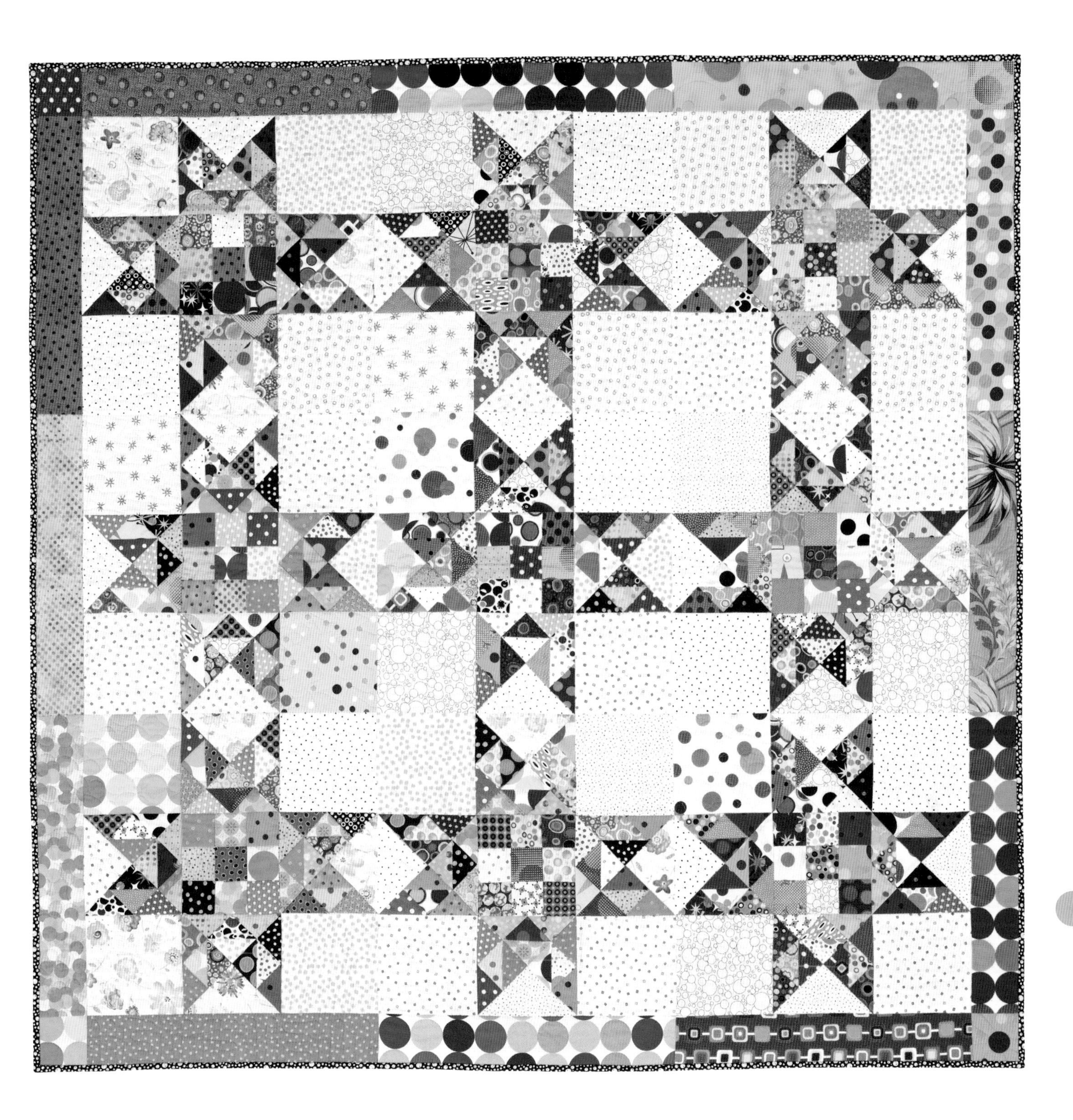

SUNSHINE AND *Shade*

Project designer Mabeth Oxenreider used reproduction fabrics and the traditional Path Thru the Woods block to create a stunning bed-size quilt.

Materials

3½ yards total of assorted dark prints for blocks, middle and outer borders, and binding

2⅜ yards total of assorted light prints for blocks

⅜ yard of bright pink print for inner border

⅝ yard of brown print for binding

3⅔ yards of backing fabric

66×82" of quilt batting

Finished quilt top: 60×76"
Finished block: 8" square

Quantities specified for 44/45"-wide, 100% cotton fabrics. All measurements include a ¼" seam allowance. Sew with right sides together unless otherwise stated.

Select the Fabrics

Designer Mabeth Oxenreider used only one dark print and one light print in each block. If you'd like a scrappier quilt, mix assorted dark prints and assorted light prints in the individual blocks.

Cut the Fabrics

To make the best use of your fabrics, cut the pieces in the order that follows.

continued

From assorted dark prints, cut:
- 30—3×18" strips for middle and outer borders
- 24—6⅞" squares, cutting each in half diagonally for a total of 48 large triangles
- 168—2⅞" squares, cutting each in half diagonally for a total of 336 small triangles

From assorted light prints, cut:
- 24—6⅞" squares, cutting each in half diagonally for a total of 48 large triangles
- 168—2⅞" squares, cutting each in half diagonally for a total of 336 small triangles

From bright pink print, cut:
- 6—1½×42" strips for inner border

From brown print, cut:
- 7—2½×42" binding strips

Assemble the Blocks

1. Sew together one dark print small triangle and one light print small triangle to make a triangle-square (see Diagram 1). Press the seam allowance toward the dark triangle. The pieced triangle-square should measure 2½" square, including the seam allowances. Repeat to make a total of four triangle-squares.

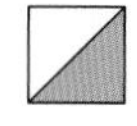

Diagram 1

2. Referring to Diagram 2 for placement, lay out the four triangle-squares, three light print small triangles, and three dark print small triangles in sections. Sew together the pieces in each section, then join the sections.

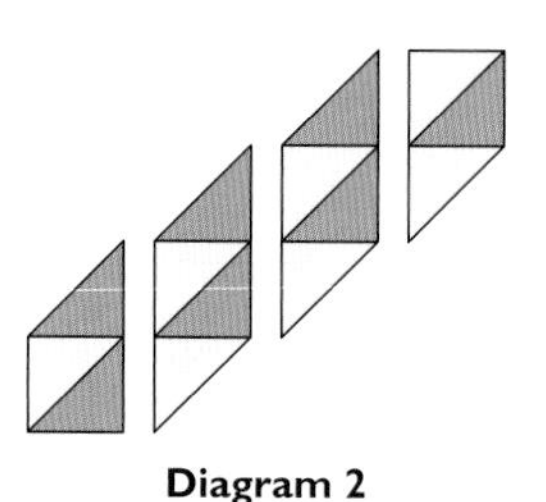

Diagram 2

3. Referring to Diagram 3, sew a light print large triangle and a dark print large triangle to the long edges of the pieced small triangles to make a block. Press the seam allowances toward the large triangles. The pieced block should measure 8½" square, including the seam allowances.

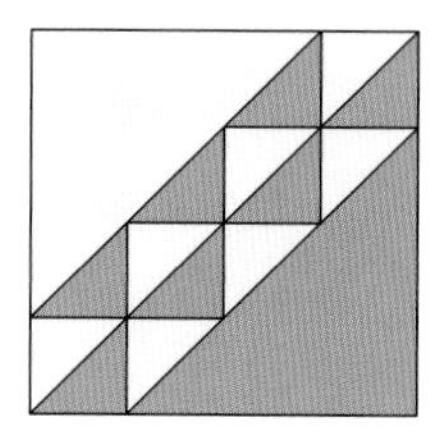

Diagram 3

4. Repeat steps 1 through 3 to make a total of 48 blocks.

Assemble the Quilt Center

1. Referring to the photograph *opposite* for placement, lay out the pieced blocks in eight horizontal rows. Sew together the blocks in each row. Press the seam allowances in one direction, alternating the direction with each row.

2. Join the rows to make the quilt center. Press the seam allowances in one direction. The pieced quilt center should measure 48½×64½", including the seam allowances.

Add the Borders

1. Cut and piece the bright pink print 1½×42" strips to make the following:
   - 2—1½×64½" inner border strips
   - 2—1½×50½" inner border strips

2. Sew the long bright pink print inner border strips to the long edges of the pieced quilt center. Then join the short bright pink print inner border strips to the short edges of the pieced quilt center. Press all seam allowances toward the inner border.

3. Cut and diagonally piece the assorted dark print 3×18" strips to make the following:
   - 2—3×71½" outer border strips
   - 2—3×60½" outer border strips
   - 2—3×66½" middle border strips
   - 2—3×55½" middle border strips

4. Sew the long dark print middle border strips to the long edges of the pieced quilt center. Then join the short dark print middle border strips to the short edges of the pieced quilt center. Press all seam allowances toward the middle border.

5. Sew the long dark print outer border strips to the long edges of the pieced quilt center. Then join the short dark print outer border strips to

the short edges of the pieced quilt center to complete the quilt top. Press all seam allowances toward the outer border.

Complete the Quilt

1. Layer the quilt top, batting, and backing according to the instructions in Quilter's Schoolhouse, which begins on *page 150*.

2. Quilt as desired. Use the brown print 2½×42" strips to bind the quilt according to the instructions in Quilter's Schoolhouse.

continued

Sunshine and Shade Quilt

optional sizes

If you'd like to make this quilt in a size other than for a lap size, use the information *below.*

Alternate quilt sizes	Crib/Lap	Full/Queen	King
Number of blocks	16	100	144
Number of blocks wide by long	4×4	10×10	12×12
Finished size	44" square	92" square	108" square
Yardage requirements			
Assorted dark prints	2 yards	5½ yards	7½ yards
Assorted light prints	1 yard	4⅓ yards	5⅞ yards
Bright pink print	¼ yard	½ yard	½ yard
Brown print	½ yard	⅞ yard	⅞ yard
Backing	2⅞ yards	8¼ yards	9½ yards
Batting	50" square	98" square	114" square

PILLOW

Reproductions of vintage ABC prints cover this playroom floor pillow.

Materials

2 yards of red print for blocks, outer border, and pillow back

¼ yard of blue print for blocks

¼ yard of yellow polka dot for blocks

¼ yard of green polka dot for blocks

⅜ yard of blue polka dot for inner border and binding

30" square of muslin for lining

30" square of quilt batting

24"-square pillow form

Finished pillow: 24" square

Cut the Fabrics

To make the best use of your fabrics, cut the pieces in the order that follows.

From red print, cut:

- 2—24½×30" rectangles
- 2—3½×24½" outer border strips
- 2—3½×18½" outer border strips
- 1—6⅞" square, cutting it in half diagonally for a total of 2 large triangles
- 7—2⅞" squares, cutting each in half diagonally for a total of 14 small triangles

From blue print, cut:

- 1—6⅞" square, cutting it in half diagonally for a total of 2 large triangles
- 7—2⅞" squares, cutting each in half diagonally for a total of 14 small triangles

From yellow polka dot, cut:
- 1—6⅞" square, cutting it in half diagonally for a total of 2 large triangles
- 7—2⅞" squares, cutting each in half diagonally for a total of 14 small triangles

From green polka dot, cut:
- 1—6⅞" square, cutting it in half diagonally for a total of 2 large triangles
- 7—2⅞" squares, cutting each in half diagonally for a total of 14 small triangles

From blue polka dot, cut:
- 3—2½x42" binding strips
- 2—1½x18½" inner border strips
- 2—1½x16½" inner border strips

Assemble the Blocks

1. Referring to the photograph *right* and Assemble the Blocks on *page 88*, steps 1 and 2, use the blue print small triangles and yellow polka-dot small triangles to make a total of eight triangle-squares. Use the triangle-squares, the remaining yellow polka-dot small triangles, and the remaining blue print small triangles to make a total of two pieced small-triangle sections.

2. Referring to Assemble the Blocks on *page 88*, Step 3, sew a blue print large triangle and yellow polka-dot large triangle to the long edges of a pieced small-triangle section to make a block. Repeat to make a second block.

3. Repeat steps 1 and 2 using the red print and green polka-dot triangles to make two blocks.

Assemble the Pillow Center

1. Referring to the photograph *above right* for placement, lay out the four blocks in pairs. Sew together the pairs. Press the seam allowances in opposite directions.

2. Join the pairs to make the pillow center. Press the seam allowance in one direction. The pieced pillow center should measure 16½" square, including the seam allowances.

Add the Borders

1. Sew the blue polka dot 1½x16½" inner border strips to opposite edges of the pillow center. Add the blue polka dot 1½x18½" inner border strips to the remaining edges of the pillow center. Press the seam allowances toward the inner border.

2. Sew the red print 3½x18½" outer border strips to opposite edges of the pillow center. Add the red print 3½x24½" outer border strips to the remaining edges to complete the pillow top. Press the seam allowances toward the outer border.

Complete the Pillow

1. Layer the pillow top, batting, and muslin lining according to instructions in Quilter's Schoolhouse, which begins on *page 150*. Quilt as desired.

2. With wrong sides inside, fold each red print 24½x30" rectangle in half to form two double-thick 15x24½" pieces. Overlap the folded edges by 6". Stitch ¼" from the top and bottom edges, including across the folds, to secure the pieces and create the pillow back.

3. With wrong sides together, layer the pillow top and the pillow back. Sew together the pieces along all four edges to make a pillow cover.

4. Use the blue polka-dot 2½x42" strips to bind the pillow cover according to the instructions in Quilter's Schoolhouse. Insert the pillow form through the back opening to complete the pillow.

WALL HANGING

Using similar-value blue and green batiks gives the sense of a deep, impenetrable ocean.

Materials

1½ yards total of assorted blue and green batiks for blocks

¼ yard of off-white print for one block

½ yard of light green batik for one block and inner border

⅓ yard of aqua batik for middle border

½ yard of dark blue batik for outer border

½ yard of blue batik for binding

1⅝ yards of backing fabric

55×39" of quilt batting

Finished quilt top: 49×33"

Cut the Fabrics

To make the best use of your fabrics, cut the pieces in the order that follows.

From assorted blue and green batiks, cut:

- 14—6⅞" squares, cutting each in half diagonally for a total of 28 large triangles
- 98—2⅞" squares, cutting each in half diagonally for a total of 196 small triangles

From off-white print, cut:

- 1—6⅞" square, cutting it in half diagonally for a total of 2 large triangles (you'll have 1 leftover large triangle)
- 4—2⅞" squares, cutting each in half diagonally for a total of 8 small triangles (you'll have 1 leftover small triangle)

From light green batik, cut:

- 2—1¼×42" inner border strips
- 2—1¼×24½" inner border strips
- 1—6⅞" square, cutting it in half diagonally for a total of 2 large triangles (you'll have 1 leftover large triangle)
- 4—2⅞" squares, cutting each in half diagonally for a total of 8 small triangles (you'll have 1 leftover small triangle)

From aqua batik, cut:

- 3—2¼×42" strips for middle border
- 2—2¼×26" middle border strips

From dark blue batik, cut:

- 3—2½×42" strips for outer border
- 2—2½×29½" outer border strips

From blue batik, cut:

- 5—2½×42" binding strips

Assemble the Blocks

1. Referring to the photograph *opposite* and Assemble the Blocks on *page 88*, steps 1 and 2, use light green batik small triangles and off-white print small triangles to make a total of four triangle-squares. Use the triangle-squares, three light green batik small triangles, and three off-white print small triangles to make a pieced small-triangle section.

2. Referring to Assemble the Blocks on *page 88*, Step 3, sew a light green batik large triangle and off-white print large triangle to the long edges of the pieced small-triangle section to make one block.

3. Repeat steps 1 and 2 using the blue and green batik small triangles and large triangles to make a total of 14 additional blocks.

Assemble the Quilt Center

1. Referring to the photograph *opposite* for placement, lay out the pieced blocks in three horizontal rows. Sew together the blocks in each row. Press the seam allowances in one direction, alternating the direction with each row.

2. Join the rows to complete the quilt center. Press the seam allowances in one direction. The pieced quilt center should measure 40½×24½", including the seam allowances.

Add the Borders

1. Sew the light green batik 1¼×24½" inner border strips to the short edges of the pieced quilt center. Add the light green batik 1¼×42" inner border strips to the long edges of the pieced quilt center. Press all seam allowances toward the inner border.

2. Cut and piece the aqua batik 2¼×42" strips to make the following:
   - 2—2¼×45½" middle border strips

3. Sew the aqua batik 2¼×26" middle border strips to the short edges of the pieced quilt center. Add the long aqua batik middle border strips to the long edges of the pieced quilt center. Press all seam allowances toward the middle border.

4. Cut and piece the dark blue batik 2½×42" strips to make the following:
   - 2—2½×49½" outer border strips

5. Sew the dark blue batik 2½×29½" outer border strips to the short edges of the pieced quilt center. Add the long dark blue batik outer border strips to the long edges of the pieced quilt center to complete the quilt top. Press all seam allowances toward the outer border.

Complete the Quilt

1. Layer the quilt top, batting, and backing according to instructions in Quilter's Schoolhouse, which begins on *page 150*. Quilt as desired.

2. Use the blue batik 2½×42" strips to bind the quilt according to the instructions in Quilter's Schoolhouse.

BITS AND PIECES

Concoct a gourmet feast for the eyes by adding a scrap of this print and a touch of that stripe to cook up your next quilt. Whether you make the playful "Centennial Pineapple," the subdued "Jacob's Ladder," or the plucky "Rule the Roost," you'll be treating yourself to a scrumptious taste testing of scrap combinations.

CENTENNIAL *Pineapple*

The Pineapple block, a variation of the Log Cabin,

shows a quilter's interpretation of the jagged edges of the tropical fruit.

Materials

1⅔ yards total of assorted cream prints for blocks

2½ yards total of assorted prints in red, blue, navy, gold, pink, olive, and brown for blocks

½ yard of blue print for binding

2⅞ yards of backing fabric

50" square of quilt batting

Finished quilt top: 44" square
Finished block: 11" square

Quantities specified for 44/45"-wide, 100% cotton fabrics. All measurements include a ¼" seam allowance. Sew with right sides together unless otherwise stated.

Cut the Fabrics

To make the best use of your fabrics, cut the pieces in the order that follows. The patterns are on *Pattern Sheet 1.* To make templates of the patterns, follow the instructions in Quilter's Schoolhouse, which begins on *page 150.*

continued

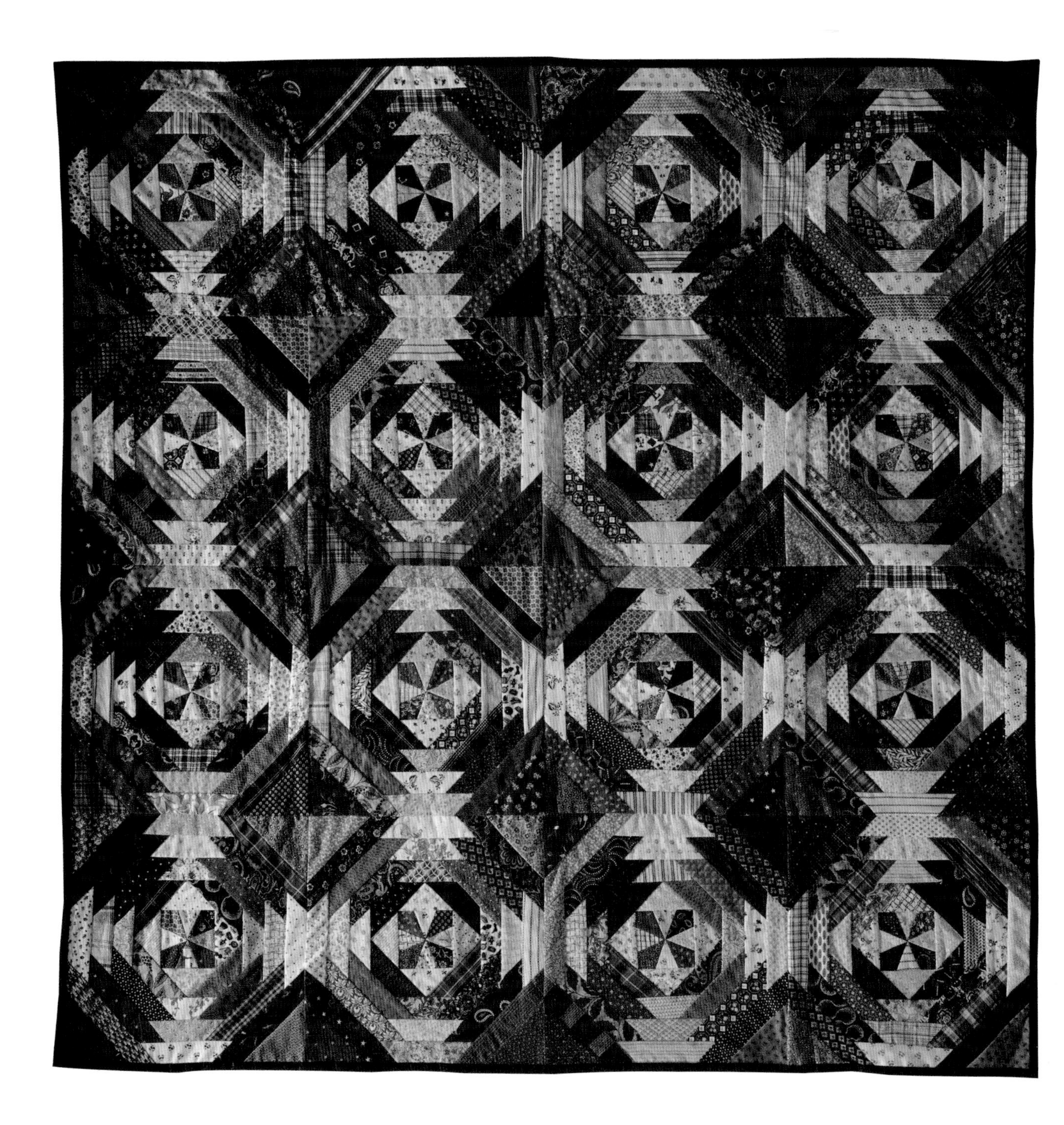

From assorted cream prints, cut:
- 64 *each* of patterns A, C, E, G, and I

From assorted red, blue, navy, gold, pink, olive, and brown prints, cut:
- 64 *each* of patterns B, D, F, H, J, and K

From blue print, cut:
- 5—2×42" binding strips

Assemble the Pinwheel Units

1. Referring to Diagram 1 for placement, sew together a cream print A triangle and a dark print B piece to make an AB unit. Press the seam allowance toward the dark print piece. Repeat to make a total of 64 AB units.

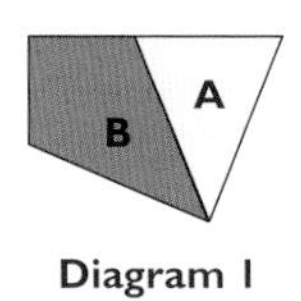

Diagram 1

2. Sew together two AB units to make a pinwheel half (see Diagram 2). Press the seam allowance toward the light print piece. Repeat to make a total of 32 pinwheel halves.

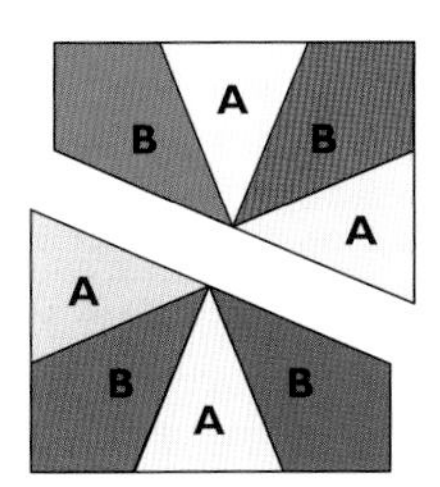

Diagram 2

3. Join two pinwheel halves to make a pinwheel unit (see Diagram 3). Press the seam allowance open. Each pinwheel unit should measure 3" square, including seam allowances. Repeat to make a total of 16 pinwheel units.

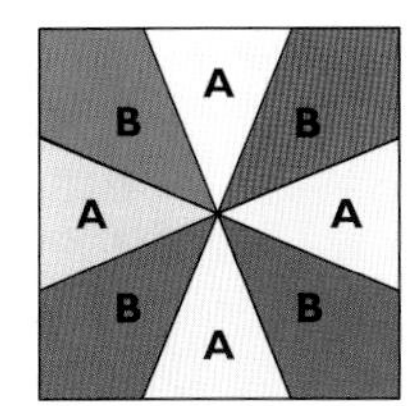

Diagram 3

Assemble the Blocks

1. Sew cream print C triangles to opposite edges of a pinwheel unit (see Diagram 4). Press the seam allowances toward the triangles. Sew cream print C triangles to the remaining edges of the pinwheel unit to make a block center. Press the seam allowances toward the triangles.

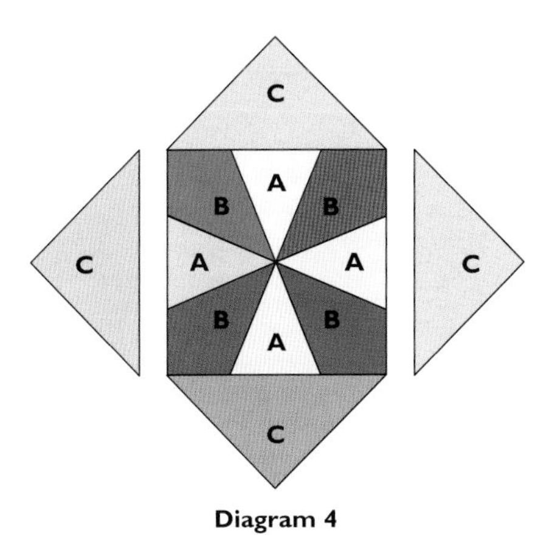

Diagram 4

2. Referring to the Block Assembly Diagram and working in alphabetical order, sew four of each remaining piece to the block center, joining them in pairs to opposite edges as in Step 1, to make a Pineapple block. Press the seam allowances away from the block center; use a pressing cloth to avoid developing a fabric "shine." The pieced Pineapple block should measure 11½" square, including the seam allowances.

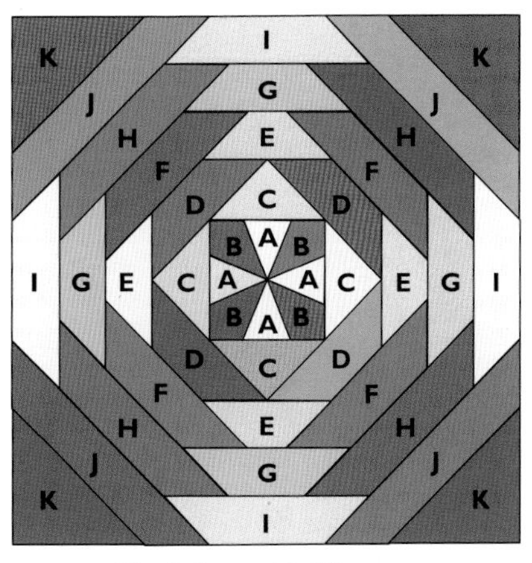

Block Assembly Diagram

3. Repeat steps 1 and 2 to make a total of 16 Pineapple blocks.

Assemble the Quilt Top

1. Referring to the photograph *opposite*, lay out the Pineapple blocks in four horizontal rows.

2. Sew together the blocks in each row. Press the seam allowances in one direction, alternating the direction with each row. Then join the rows to complete the quilt top. Press the seam allowances in one direction.

Complete the Quilt

1. Layer the quilt top, batting, and backing according to the instructions in Quilter's Schoolhouse, which begins on *page 150*. Quilt as desired.

2. Use the blue print 2×42" strips to bind the quilt according to the instructions in Quilter's Schoolhouse.

continued

Centennial Pineapple Quilt

optional sizes

If you'd like to make this quilt in a size other than for a wall hanging, use the information *below*.

Alternate quilt sizes	Lap	Full/Queen	King
Number of blocks	40	72	100
Number of blocks wide by long	5×8	8×9	10×10
Finished size	55×88"	88×99"	110" square
Yardage requirements			
Assorted cream prints	3⅛ yards	5½ yards	7½ yards
Assorted prints in red, blue, navy, gold, pink, olive, and brown	4¾ yards	8½ yards	11⅝ yards
Blue print	⅝ yard	⅔ yard	¾ yard
Backing	5¼ yards	7⅞ yards	9⅔ yards
Batting	61×94"	94×105"	116" square

optional colors

Designer Judy Martin made a striking reproduction of her "Centennial Pineapple" quilt in blue and white. The placement of the contrasting fabric emphasizes the pointed edges of the pieces in this quilt.

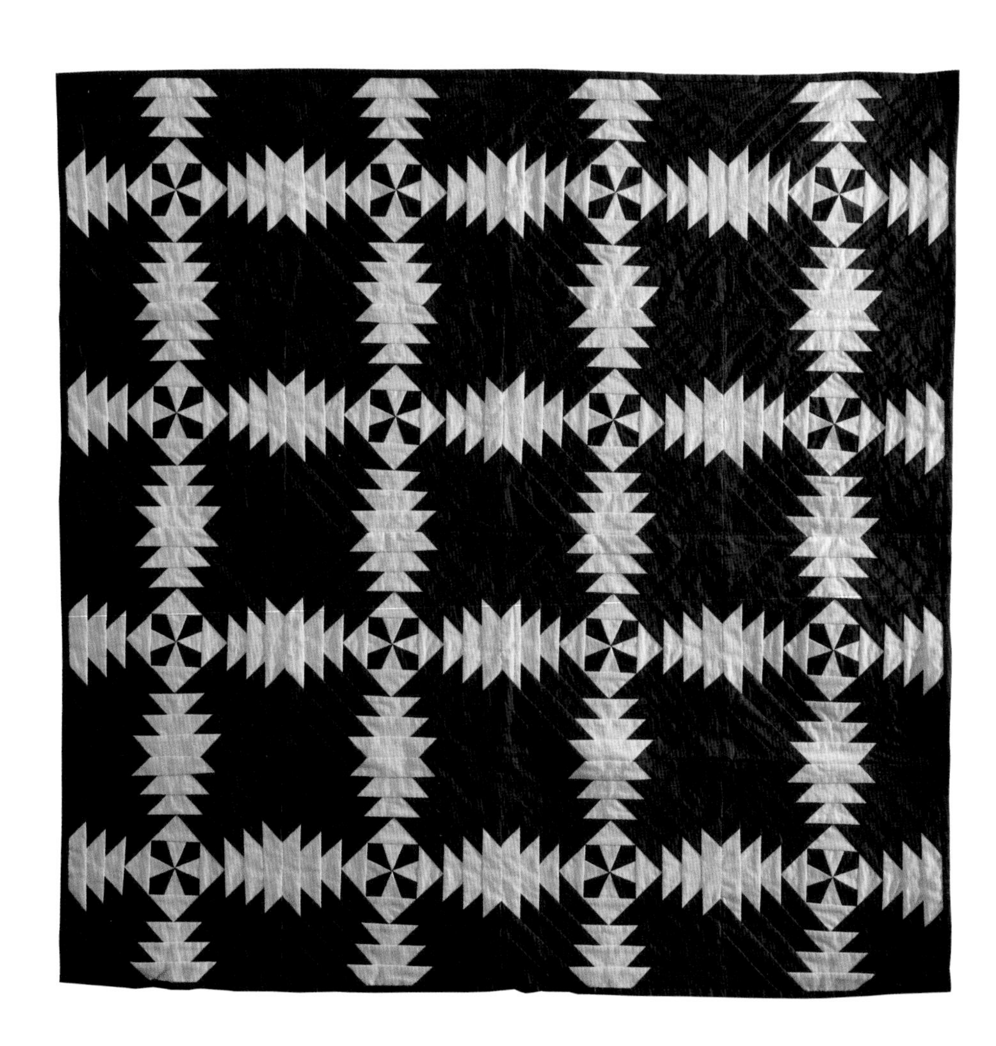

PILLOW

Yellow and green prints give the Pineapple block pillow a Caribbean flair.

Materials

¼ yard of yellow print for pillow top

⅓ yard of green print for pillow top

⅜ yard of yellow-and-green print for backing

15" square of muslin for lining

15" square of quilt batting

11"-square pillow form

⅞"-diameter button

Finished pillow: 11" square

Cut the Fabrics

To make the best use of your fabrics, cut the pieces in the order that follows. This project uses "Centennial Pineapple" patterns on *Pattern Sheet 1*. To make templates of the patterns, follow the instructions in Quilter's Schoolhouse, which begins on *page 150*.

From yellow print, cut:
- 4 *each* of patterns A, C, E, G, and I

From green print, cut:
- 4 *each* of patterns B, D, F, H, J, and K

From yellow-and-green print, cut:
- 2—11½×14½" rectangles

Assemble the Pillow Top

1. Referring to Assemble the Pinwheel Units on *page 98*, use the green print B pieces and yellow print A pieces to make a pinwheel unit.

2. Referring to Assemble the Blocks on *page 99*, steps 1 and 2, use the green print D, F, H, J, and K pieces and the yellow print C, E, G, and I pieces to make a Pineapple block for the pillow top.

Complete the Pillow

1. Layer the pieced pillow top, batting, and muslin lining according to the instructions in Quilter's Schoolhouse, which begins on *page 150*. Quilt as desired. Sew the button to the center of the pillow top. Trim the batting and backing even with the pillow top edges.

2. With wrong sides inside, fold the yellow-and-green print 11½×14½" rectangles in half to form two double-thick 7¼×11½" pieces. Overlap the folded edges by 3". Stitch ¼" from the top and bottom edges, including across the folds, to secure the pieces and create the pillow back.

3. With right sides together, layer the pillow top with the pillow back. Sew together the pieces along all four edges; turn right side out. Insert the pillow form through the back opening to complete the pillow.

TREE SKIRT

Encircle your Christmas tree with a skirt bedecked with festive Pineapple blocks.

Materials

⅞ yard total of assorted red prints for blocks

⅞ yard total of assorted green prints for blocks

1 yard total of assorted cream prints for blocks

2½ yards of dark red print for tree skirt and ties

1⅛ yards of muslin for block backings

Finished tree skirt: 52" in diameter (point to point)

Cut the Fabrics

To make the best use of your fabrics, cut the pieces in the order that follows. This project uses "Centennial Pineapple" patterns and the Tree Skirt Arc Pattern on *Pattern Sheet 1*. To make templates of the patterns, follow the instructions in Quilter's Schoolhouse, which begins on *page 150*.

From assorted red prints, cut:
- 16 *each* of patterns B, D, F, H, J, and K

From assorted green prints, cut:
- 16 *each* of patterns B, D, F, H, J, and K

From assorted cream prints, cut:
- 32 *each* of patterns A, C, E, G, and I

From dark red print, cut:
- 2—42" squares
- 1—1½×30" strip

From muslin, cut:
- 8—11½" squares

Assemble the Blocks

1. Referring to the Block Assembly Diagram *below* and Assemble the Pinwheel Units on *page 98*, use two red print B pieces, two green print B pieces, and four cream print A pieces to make one pinwheel unit. Repeat to make a total of eight pinwheel units.

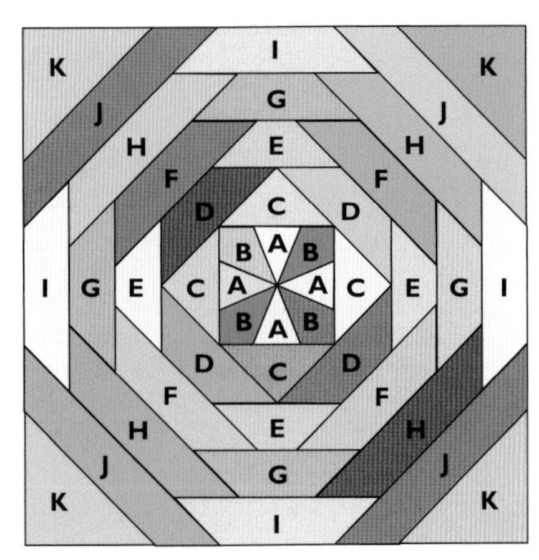

Block Assembly Diagram

2. Referring to the Block Assembly Diagram *above* and Assemble the Blocks on *page 99*, steps 1 and 2, use two each of the green print D, F, H, J, and K pieces, two each of the red print D, F, H, J, and K pieces, and four each of the cream print C, E, G, and I pieces to make a Pineapple block. Repeat to make a total of eight Pineapple blocks.

Complete the Tree Skirt

1. With right sides together, layer a pieced block with a muslin 11½" square; sew together, leaving a 3" opening for turning. Turn right side out; press. Hand-stitch the opening closed. Repeat with the remaining blocks and muslin square.

2. With right sides together, fold a dark red print 42" square in half horizontally, to make a rectangle. Fold the rectangle in half to make a square. Using the Arc Pattern and the Tree Skirt Cutting Diagram on *Pattern Sheet 1*, cut the folded square along the curved edge of the arc pattern to make a circle for the tree skirt top. Repeat with the other dark red print 42" square to make the tree skirt back.

3. With right sides together, layer the tree skirt top and back circles. Cut a straight slit from the center of the layered circles to the outer edge. Cut a 5"-diameter circle in the center.

4. Sew together the layered circles along all edges, leaving a 3" opening along a straight edge for turning. Clip across the seam allowances at the corners; around the center circle, clip through the seam allowance to the seam line every ½". Turn the stitched circles right side out; press. Hand-stitch the opening closed to complete the tree skirt base.

5. Lay the tree skirt base on a flat surface. Referring to the photograph *below*, position the pieced blocks on the tree skirt base. The pieced blocks will extend 6" beyond the outer edge of the tree skirt base. Topstitch the blocks in place, leaving each lower edge free.

6. With the wrong side inside, fold the long edges of the red print 1½×30" strip so they meet at the center; press. Cut the strip into two 15" lengths. Fold the short edges ¼" to the inside; press. Then fold the strips in half lengthwise; press. Topstitch along the strip's long and short edges to make the ties. Stitch the ties to the tree skirt at the center circle opening to complete the tree skirt.

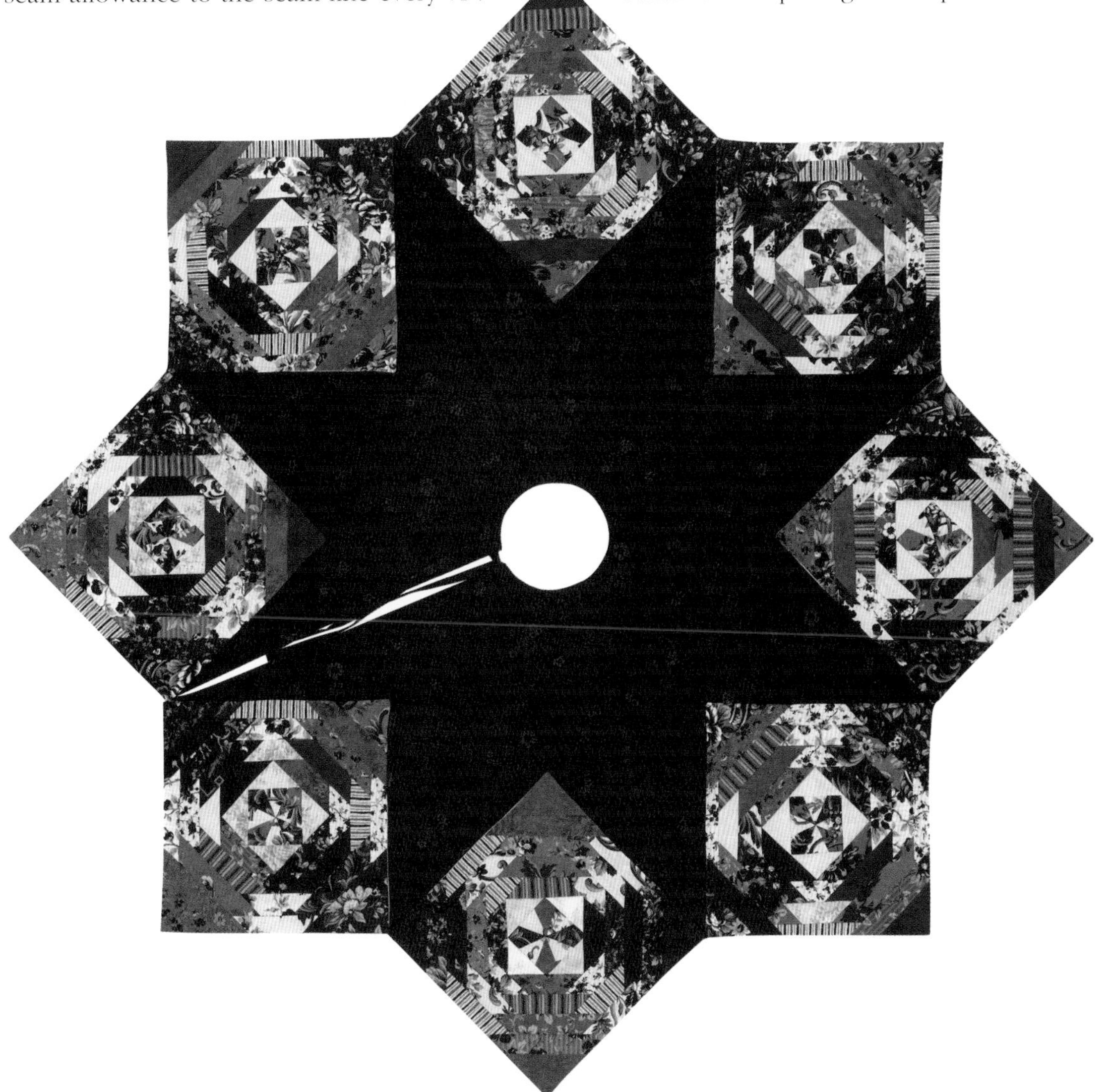

JACOB'S *Ladder*

When this small-scale version of a classic pattern caught the eye of quilt collector Mary Ellen Von Holt, she purchased it for her collection. With the reproduction 1930s fabrics available today, you can make a new "antique" quilt.

Materials

⅞ yard of solid yellow for blocks

⅞ yard of solid green for blocks

1⅞ yards total of assorted solids and prints for blocks

⅓ yard of green print for binding

37×46" of backing fabric

37×46" of thin quilt batting

Finished quilt top: 33×42"
Finished block: 3" square

Quantities specified for 44/45"-wide, 100% cotton fabrics. All measurements include a ¼" seam allowance. Sew with right sides together unless otherwise stated.

Designer Notes

Mary Ellen Von Holt, who has collected antique doll quilts for more than two decades, particularly appreciates the scale of these little quilts.

"The scale on a doll or crib quilt is smaller than a larger quilt," she says. For example, a finished Nine-Patch unit might be 3" square in a crib quilt instead of 6" square.

Cut the Fabrics

To make the best use of your fabrics, cut the pieces in the order that follows.

continued

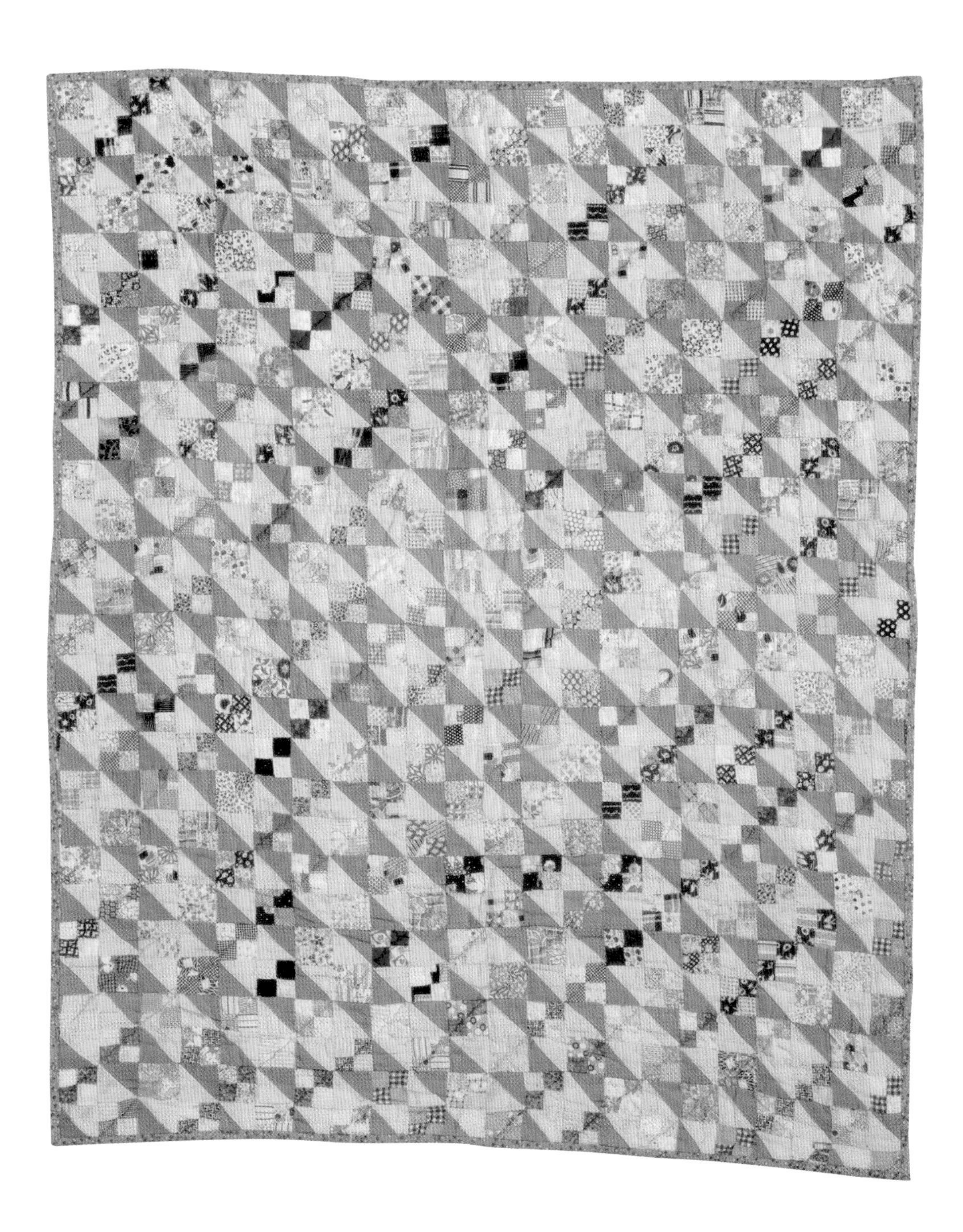

From solid yellow, cut:

- 154—2⅜" squares, cutting each in half diagonally for a total of 308 triangles

From solid green, cut:

- 154—2⅜" squares, cutting each in half diagonally for a total of 308 triangles

From assorted solids and prints, cut:

- 78—1¼×21" strips

From green print, cut:

- 4—2¼×42" binding strips

Assemble the Jacob's Ladder Blocks

1. Sew together a solid yellow triangle and a solid green triangle to make a triangle-square (see Diagram 1). Press the seam allowance toward the solid green triangle. The pieced triangle-square should measure 2" square, including the seam allowances. Repeat to make a total of 308 triangle-squares.

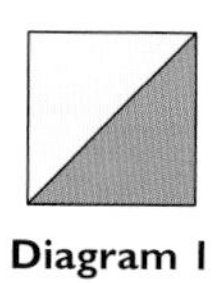

Diagram 1

2. Join two assorted 1¼×21" strips to make a strip set (see Diagram 2). Press the seam allowance toward the darker print. Repeat to make a total of 39 strip sets. Cut the strip sets into 1¼"-wide segments for a total of 616.

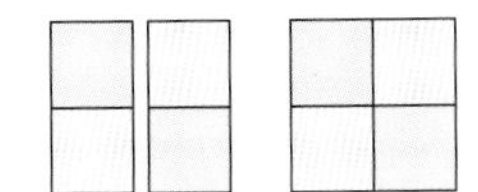

Diagram 2

3. Sew together two 1¼"-wide segments to make a Four-Patch unit (see Diagram 3). Press the seam allowance in one direction. The pieced Four-Patch unit should measure 2" square, including the seam allowances.

Diagram 3

4. Repeat Step 3 to make a total of 308 Four-Patch units.

5. Referring to Diagram 4 for placement, sew together two triangle-squares and two Four-Patch units in pairs. Press the seam allowances toward the triangle-squares. Then join the pairs to make a Jacob's Ladder block. Press the seam allowances in one direction. The pieced Jacob's Ladder block should measure 3½" square, including the seam allowances. Repeat to make a total of 154 Jacob's Ladder blocks.

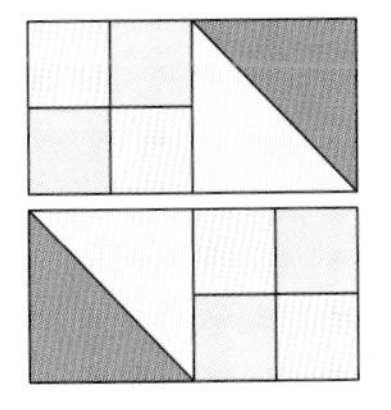

Diagram 4

Assemble the Quilt Top

1. Referring to the photograph *opposite* for placement, lay out the Jacob's Ladder blocks in 14 horizontal rows.

2. Sew together the blocks in each row. Press the seam allowances in one direction, alternating the direction with each row. Then join the rows to complete the quilt top. Press the seam allowances in one direction.

Complete the Quilt

1. Layer the quilt top, batting, and backing according to the instructions in Quilter's Schoolhouse, which begins on *page 150*.

2. Quilt as desired. This quilt was hand-quilted in the ditch of every seam.

3. Use the green print 2¼×42" strips to bind the quilt according to the instructions in Quilter's Schoolhouse.

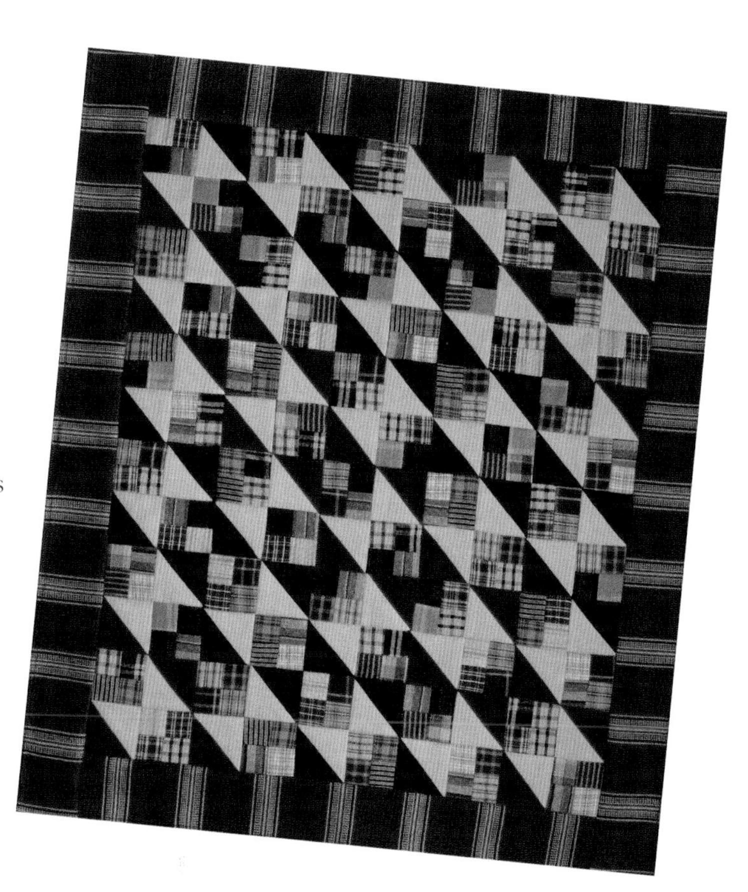

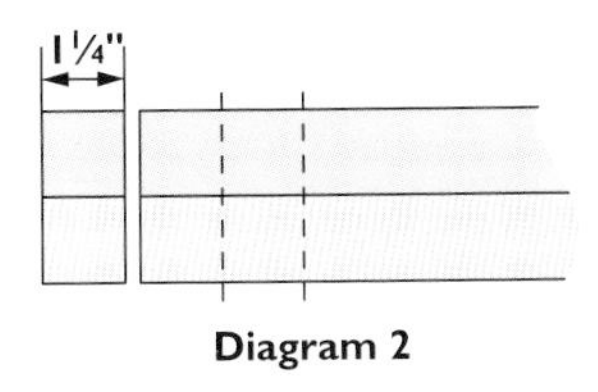

optional colors

"I wanted to keep the old look of the original quilt, maybe even go a bit more primitive," quilt tester Laura Boehnke says. She used red and black to make the secondary stars stand out. "That way, you can create a design within a design," she says.

TOTE BAG

Put together a purse as sweet as a summer watermelon for yourself or a friend.

Materials

18×22" piece (fat quarter) of pink print for blocks, band, and bag base

18×22" piece (fat quarter) of dark pink print for blocks and lining

¼ yard of light green print for blocks

¼ yard of green print for blocks and bag handle

⅛ yard of green polka dot for blocks

⅓ yard of muslin for backing

16×26" of thin quilt batting

3×9" rectangle of heavy cardboard

Finished bag: 9" wide, 9" high, and 3" deep

Cut the Fabrics

To make the best use of your fabrics, cut the pieces in the order that follows.

From pink print, cut:
- 1—3½×9½" rectangle for bottom
- 2—2×12½" rectangles for band
- 20—2⅜" squares, cutting each in half diagonally for a total of 40 triangles

From dark pink print, cut:
- 2—9½×12½" rectangles for lining
- 1—3½×9½" rectangle for lining
- 20—2⅜" squares, cutting each in half diagonally for a total of 40 triangles

From light green print, cut:
- 4—1¼×42" strips

From green print, cut:
- 2—1¼×42" strips
- 2—2×18½" strips for handles

From green polka dot, cut:
- 2—1¼×42" strips

From muslin, cut:
- 2—9½×12½" rectangles
- 1—3½×9½" rectangle

From thin quilt batting, cut:
- 2—9½×12½" rectangles
- 1—3½×9½" rectangle

Assemble the Bag Front and Back

1. Referring to the photograph *left* and Assemble the Jacob's Ladder Blocks on *page 106*, Step 1, use the pink print triangles and dark pink print triangles to make a total of 40 triangle-squares.

2. Referring to the photograph and Assemble the Jacob's Ladder Blocks, steps 2 and 3, use the light green print and green print 1¼×42" strips to make a total of 20 Four-Patch units. Use the remaining light green print and green polka dot 1¼×42" strips to make a total of 20 Four-Patch units.

3. Referring to Diagram 5 and the photograph, sew together the triangle-squares and Four-Patch units in two groups of five horizontal rows each. Note how the Four-Patch units are placed to create diagonal rows of the same units. Add a pink print 2×12½" rectangle to the top edge of each block group to make the bag front and back.

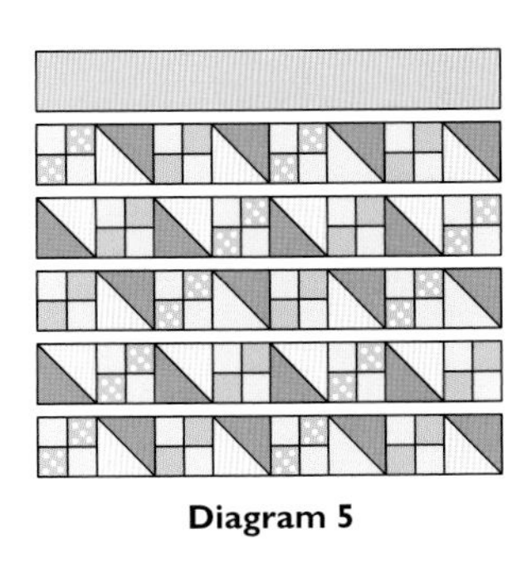

Diagram 5

Assemble the Outer Bag

1. Layer the bag front with batting and muslin 9½x12½" rectangles. Baste the three layers together a scant ¼" from all edges. Quilt as desired. Repeat with the bag back.

2. Layer the pink print 3½x9½" rectangle with batting and muslin 3½x9½" rectangles. Baste the three layers together a scant ¼" from all edges to make the bag base. Quilt as desired.

3. Mark the center bottom of the bag front and back; mark the center of each long edge of the bag base (see Diagram 6).

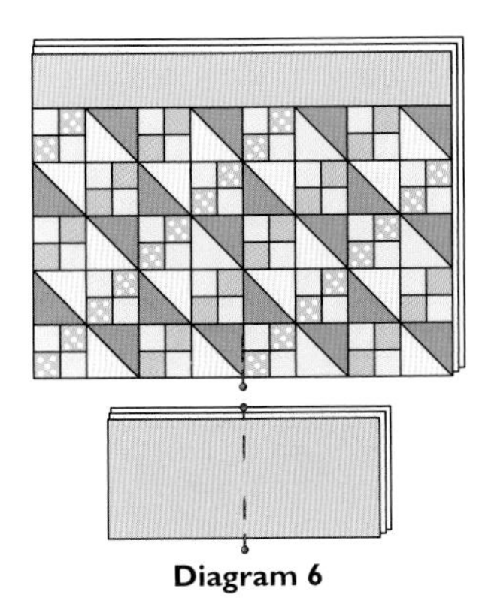

Diagram 6

4. Matching the centers, sew the bag base to the bag front and back (see Diagram 7). Press the seam allowances toward the bag base. Topstitch the bag base through all layers, about ⅛" from the seams.

5. Fold a green print 2x18½" strip in half lengthwise with the right side inside; stitch along the long edge. Trim the seam allowance to ⅛". Turn right side out and press flat. Topstitch ⅛" from the long edges to make a strap. Repeat to make a second strap.

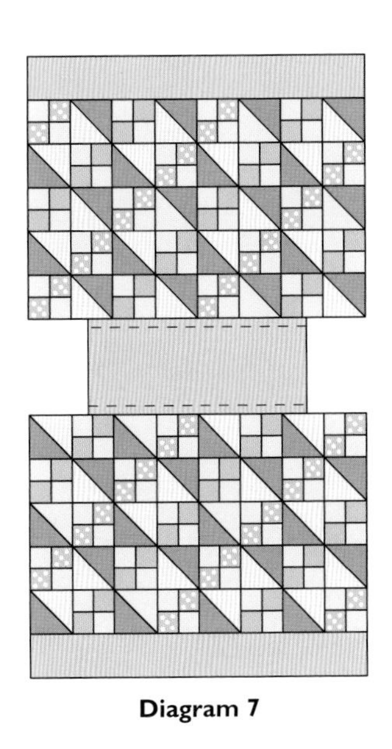

Diagram 7

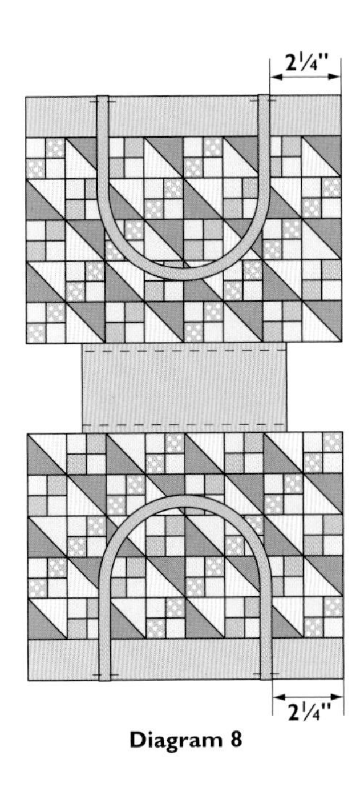

Diagram 8

6. Referring to Diagram 8, pin a bag handle to the top of the bag front and the bag back with the ends about 2¼" from the side edges; baste.

7. Pin the bag front to the bag back; sew together. Press the seam allowances open. Mark the center of a short edge of the bag base with a pin. Fold the bag so the pin matches the corresponding side seam (see Diagram 9). Stitch across the end of the bag. Repeat with the other side of the bag to complete the outer bag.

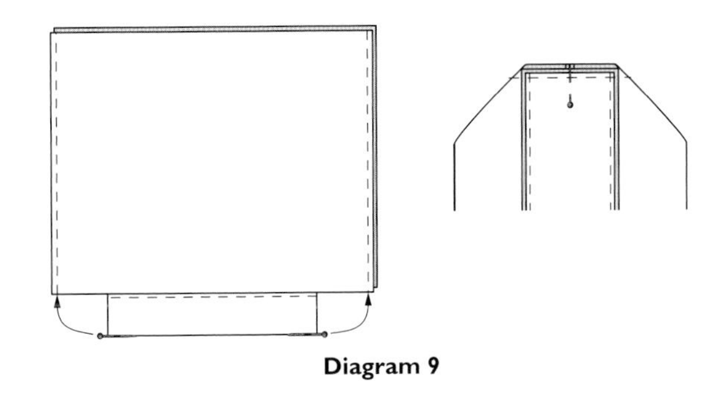

Diagram 9

Assemble the Bag Lining

1. Mark the center bottom of the dark pink print 9½x12½" rectangles. Mark the center of each long edge of the dark pink print 3½x9½" rectangle. Matching the centers, sew the large rectangles to the small rectangle to make the bag lining; press the seam allowances toward the small rectangle. Topstitch the small rectangle through all layers about ⅛" from the seams.

continued

2. Sew together the bag lining sides, leaving an opening for turning on one side. Press the seam allowances open. Mark the center of a short side of the bag lining base with a pin. Fold the lining so that the pin matches the corresponding side seam (see Diagram 10). Stitch across the end of the lining. Repeat with the other side of the lining.

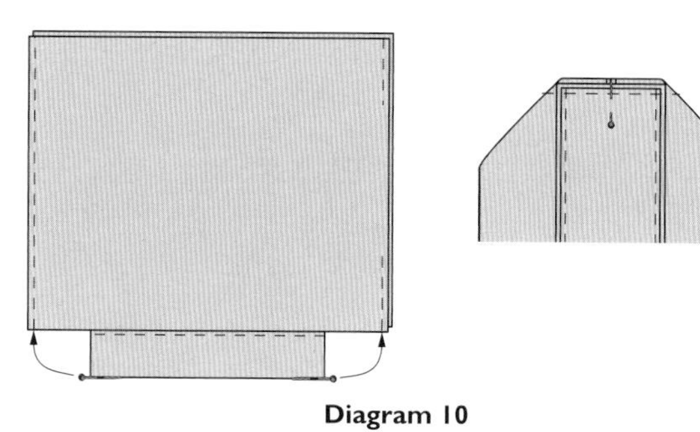

Diagram 10

Complete the Bag

1. Place lining inside outer bag with right sides together and side seams matching. Stitch along the top edges. Turn the bag right side out through the opening in the bag lining. Slip-stitch the opening closed. Smooth the lining inside the bag. Press the bag's upper edge and topstitch ⅛" from the upper edge.

2. Place the cardboard 3×9" rectangle in the bottom of the bag.

TABLE TOPPER

Careful color placement causes a lattice pattern to appear on this table topper.

Materials

⅓ yard of red print for blocks and binding

¼ yard of gold floral for blocks

⅜ yard total of assorted prints for blocks

⅝ yard of backing fabric

24×21" of quilt batting

Finished quilt top: 18×15"

Cut the Fabrics

To make the best use of your fabrics, cut the pieces in the order that follows.

From red print, cut:

- 2—2½×42" binding strips
- 30—2⅜" squares, cutting each in half diagonally for a total of 60 triangles

From gold floral, cut:

- 30—2⅜" squares, cutting each in half diagonally for a total of 60 triangles

From assorted prints, cut:

- 16—1¼×21" strips

Assemble the Jacob's Ladder Blocks

Referring to the photograph *above* and Assemble the Jacob's Ladder Blocks on *page 106*, use the red print triangles, gold floral triangles, and assorted print 1¼×21" strips to make a total of 30 Jacob's Ladder blocks.

Assemble the Quilt Top

1. Referring to the photograph *above*, lay out the pieced blocks in five horizontal rows. Sew together the blocks in each row. Press the seam allowances in one direction, alternating the direction with each row.

2. Join the rows to complete the quilt top. Press the seam allowances in one direction.

Complete the Quilt

1. Layer the quilt top, batting, and backing according to the instructions in Quilter's Schoolhouse, which begins on *page 150*. Quilt as desired.

2. Use the red print 2½×42" strips to bind the quilt according to the instructions in Quilter's Schoolhouse.

RULE THE *Roost*

Foundation piecing makes it possible to combine multiple tiny pieces into Crow's Foot, Sunburst, and rooster blocks for a top o' the morning wall hanging designed by Mary Jo Hiney.

Materials

Scraps of assorted red, dark red, rust, gold, brown, teal, black, gray, olive green, and orange prints for rooster and Crow's Foot blocks

8—⅛-yard pieces of assorted off-white prints for rooster and Crow's Foot blocks

8—1¼×42" strips of assorted light tan prints for blocks

Scraps of assorted coral, light yellow, gold, dark gold, and orange prints for Sunburst blocks

Scraps of assorted light to medium sky blue prints for Sunburst blocks

1⅓ yards of backing fabric

34×47" of quilt batting

Lightweight, nonwoven interfacing

Black, 05 point Pigma Micron pen

Finished quilt top: 28×40¼"
Finished rooster and Crow's Foot blocks: 8" square
Finished Sunburst block: 4" square

Quantities specified for 44/45"-wide, 100% cotton fabrics. All measurements include a ¼" seam allowance. Sew with right sides together unless otherwise stated.

continued

Foundation-Piecing Method

This assembly technique requires foundation patterns of interfacing (or muslin) and fabric pieces that are at least ¼" larger on all sides than the areas they are to cover. The fabric pieces are sewn directly to the foundation patterns. *Note:* Cutting generous fabric pieces will reduce the chance for assembly errors.

Because the foundation patterns provide support, there's no need to consider grain lines when cutting fabric pieces. And the fabric pieces don't have to be cut perfectly.

To foundation-piece a block, first layer two fabric pieces with right sides together. With the right side of the foundation pattern facing up, place the layered fabric pieces under the designated area with edges a scant ¼" beyond the first stitching line. Then, with the foundation pattern still on top, stitch on the shared line that joins the two designated areas, sewing through all three layers. Press the pieces open from the fabric side and trim them to ¼" beyond the next stitching line. Continue adding pieces in numerical order until the unit is completed.

Designer Notes

Quiltmaker Mary Jo Hiney prefers using the lightest-weight nonwoven interfacing (not fusible) she can find for foundation piecing, making it unnecessary to trim it away from completed blocks. She likes to use a black .05 Pigma Micron pen and a clear ruler to trace the patterns onto the interfacing. These instructions utilize interfacing for the foundation patterns; you can substitute muslin if you wish.

Make the Foundation Patterns

1. Using a fine-point black Pigma Micron pen and a ruler, trace the patterns, which are on *Pattern Sheet 1*, onto interfacing as designated *below*. Transfer all lines and markings and leave at least ½" between tracings.

- 4 *each* of Rooster Block units A, B, C, D, E, F, and G
- 4 *each* of Rooster Block units A reversed, B reversed, C reversed, D reversed, E reversed, F reversed, and G reversed
- 16 *each* of Crow's Foot Block units A and B
- 3 of Sunburst Block
- 3 of Sunburst Block reversed

2. Cut apart the tracings, cutting ¼" from the outer seam lines, to create the foundation patterns.

Select the Fabrics

While Mary Jo used scraps of assorted prints (see the photograph *opposite*), she determined the color of each rooster body before she started sewing. To do this, she sorted her prints for the roosters into eight different color groups: dark red, red, rust, orange, teal, black, brown, and gold.

When she assembled a rooster block, she used one color for the rooster body, such as dark red, then utilized assorted brighter colors for the tail, beak, and other features. Mary Jo used eight to 10 different fabrics for each rooster and a different off-white print for each rooster block background.

For the Crow's Foot blocks she combined the assorted red, dark red, rust, and gold prints used in the rooster blocks with olive green prints. For the Sunburst blocks' backgrounds, she used sky blue prints in values ranging from light to medium.

Assemble the Blocks

Following the steps outlined in Foundation-Piecing Method on *page 114* and referring to the photograph *opposite* and the Rooster Block Assembly Diagram for color placement, cut out the fabric pieces and use the foundation patterns to assemble the individual units or blocks.

Some preseaming (first sewing together two pieces, then sewing them to the foundation as one piece) is required. In all cases, the preseamed seam is marked on the pattern with a //.

Rooster Blocks

1. Foundation-piece one each of units A, B, C, D, E, F, and G, sewing together the pieces in numerical order and preseaming unit F as indicated; press. Stitch around the outer edge of each unit's stitching line but within the ¼" seam allowance. Trim each unit on the outer traced line (as for Crow's Foot blocks).

2. Sew together units A, B, C, D, and E in alphabetical order (see the Rooster Block Assembly Diagram), matching the dots. Then sew Unit F to Unit G; add the F/G unit to Unit E to make a block center. Press all seam allowances open.

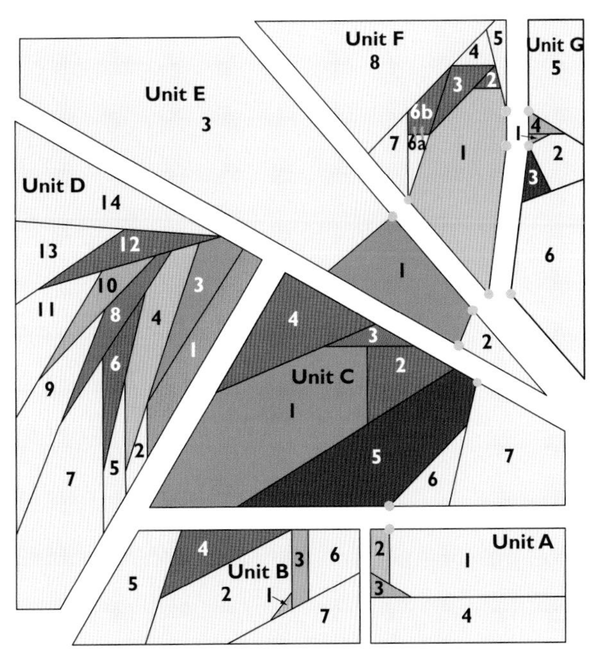

Rooster Block Assembly Diagram

continued

3. Repeat steps 1 and 2 to make a total of eight block centers. Half the block centers will be mirror images of the other half.

4. From assorted red and green print scraps, cut:
   - 16—¾×7" border strips
   - 16—¾×6½" border strips

5. Sew short red or green print border strips to opposite edges of a block center. Sew long border strips in the same red or green print to the remaining edges of a block center. Press the seam allowances toward the red or green print border. Repeat with the remaining red and green print border strips and the remaining block centers.

6. From the light tan print 1¼×42" strips, cut:
   - 16—1¼×8½" sashing strips
   - 16—1¼×7" sashing strips

7. Sew short light tan print sashing strips to opposite edges of a block center. Sew long light tan print sashing strips to the remaining edges of a block center to make a rooster block. Press the seam allowances toward the light tan print sashing. The pieced rooster block should measure 8½" square, including the seam allowances. Repeat to make a total of eight rooster blocks.

Crow's Foot Blocks

1. Foundation-piece one each of units A and B, sewing together the pieces in numerical order and preseaming as indicated in the Crow's Foot Block Assembly Diagram; press. Stitch around the outer edge of each unit but within the ¼" seam allowance. Trim each unit on the outer traced line. Sew together units A and B, matching the dots, to make a Crow's Foot subunit; press. Repeat to make a total of four Crow's Foot subunits.

2. Sew together the subunits in pairs. Then join the pairs to make a Crow's Foot block. The Crow's Foot block should measure 8½" square, including the seam allowances.

3. Repeat steps 1 and 2 to make a total of four Crow's Foot blocks.

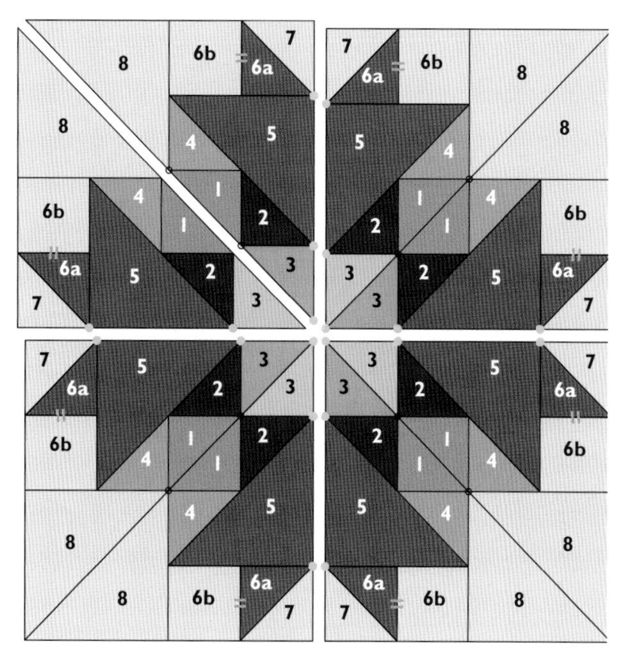

Crow's Foot Block Assembly Diagram

Sunburst Blocks

1. Foundation-piece one Sunburst block, sewing together the pieces in numerical order and preseaming as indicated on the pattern; press.

2. Using the same fabrics in the same positions as for the block pieced in Step 1, foundation-piece a reverse Sunburst block. The reverse block should be a mirror image of the Step 1 block.

3. Repeat steps 1 and 2 to make a total of three Sunburst blocks and three reverse Sunburst blocks.

Assemble the Quilt Center

1. Referring to the photograph on *page 114*, lay out the Sunburst blocks in a horizontal row, placing those with the lightest blue backgrounds in the center of the row and those with the darkest backgrounds on the ends of the row. Join the row of blocks. Press all the seam allowances open. The pieced Sunburst block row should measure 4½×24½", including seam allowances.

2. Piece gold print scraps into a ¾×24½" sashing strip. Sew the sashing strip to the bottom edge of the Sunburst block row.

3. Referring to the photograph on *page 114*, lay out the rooster and Crow's Foot blocks in four horizontal rows. Sew together the blocks in rows. Join the rows, adding the Sunburst block row to the top, to make the quilt center. Press all the seam allowances open. The pieced quilt center should measure 24½×36¾", including the seam allowances.

Assemble and Add the Borders

1. Referring to the photograph on *page 114*, cut and piece the remaining assorted print scraps to make the following:
   - 2—1×40¾" fourth border strips
   - 2—1×27½" fourth border strips
   - 2—1¼×40" third border strips
   - 2—1¼×26" third border strips
   - 2—1×38¼" second border strips
   - 2—1×25" second border strips
   - 2—¾×37¼" first border strips
   - 2—¾×24½" first border strips

2. Sew the short first border strips to the short edges of the quilt center; press the seam allowances toward the first border. Sew the long first border strips to the long edges of the quilt center; press.

3. Repeat Step 2 to add the second, third, and fourth border strips to the quilt center to complete the quilt top.

Complete the Quilt

1. Layer the quilt top, batting, and backing according to the instructions in Quilter's Schoolhouse, which begins on *page 150*.

2. Quilt as desired. Mary Jo Hiney machine-quilted her wall hanging with a meandering stitch on the rooster and Crow's Foot blocks. In the Sunburst blocks she quilted lines along the rays. She quilted a decorative wavy pattern in the borders.

3. Cut and piece the remaining red print scraps into 2×42" binding strips and bind the quilt according to the instructions in Quilter's Schoolhouse.

FRAMED ART

A scrappy rooster block adds country charm to your kitchen without the morning noise.

Materials

Scraps of assorted blue, tan, green, purple, gold, and red prints for block

⅛ yard of cream print for block

⅛ yard of red print for block and outer border

15" square of backing fabric

15" square of quilt batting

Lightweight, nonwoven interfacing

Black, 05 point Pigma Micron pen

Finished quilt top: 9½" square

Cut the Fabrics

To make the best use of your fabrics, cut the pieces in the order that follows. This project uses "Rule the Roost" Rooster Block patterns, which are on *Pattern Sheet 1*. Refer to Make the Foundation Patterns on *page 115* to create the foundation pattern.

continued

For block, trace:

- 1 *each* of Rooster Block units A, B, C, D, E, F, and G

Assemble the Quilt Top

1. Referring to Assemble the Blocks, Rooster Blocks, on *page 115*, steps 1 and 2, foundation-piece one rooster block center.

2. From gold print scraps, cut:
- 2—¾×7" inner border strips
- 2—¾×6½" inner border strips

3. Sew the short inner border strips to opposite edges of the block center. Sew the long inner border strips to the remaining edges of the block center. Press the seam allowances toward the inner border.

4. From red print, cut:
- 2—2×10" outer border strips
- 2—2×7" outer border strips

5. Sew the short outer border strips to opposite edges of the block center. Sew the long outer border strips to the remaining edges of the block center to complete the quilt top. Press the seam allowances toward the outer border.

Complete the Quilt

1. Layer the quilt top, batting, and backing according to the instructions in Quilter's Schoolhouse, which begins on *page 150*.

2. Quilt and frame the piece as desired.

TABLE RUNNER

Bustling bees fly between Crow's Foot blocks set on point in this table runner.

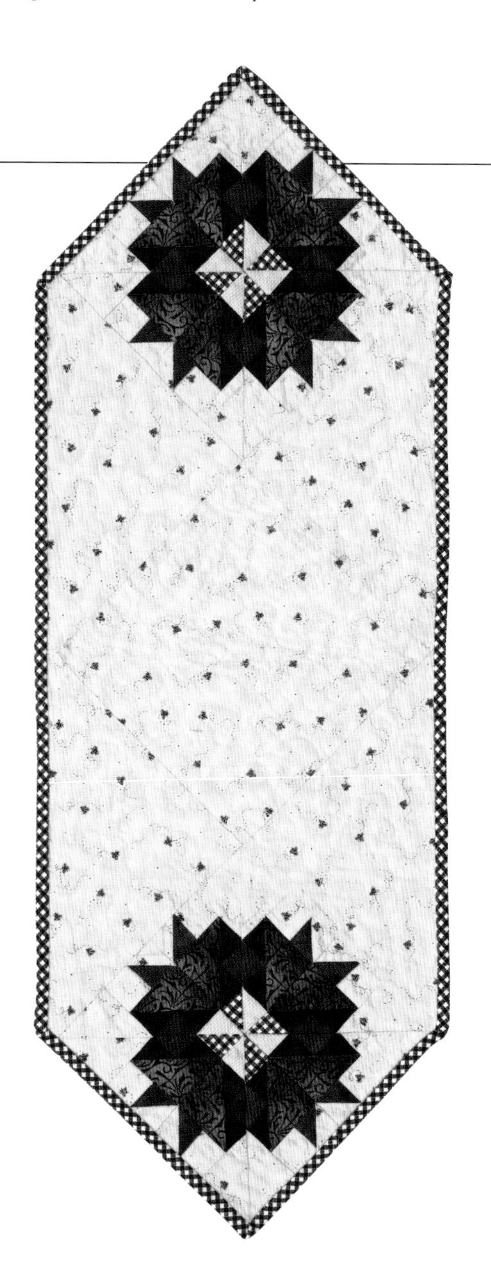

Materials

½ yard of yellow print for blocks, setting square, and setting triangles

Scraps of assorted black, brown, blue, orange, and yellow prints for blocks

¼ yard of black-and-white print for blocks and binding

½ yard of backing fabric

18×41" of quilt batting

Lightweight, nonwoven interfacing

Black, 05 point Pigma Micron pen

Finished table runner: 11⅜×34⅛"

Cut the Fabrics

To make the best use of your fabrics, cut the pieces in the order that follows. This project uses "Rule the Roost" Crow's Foot Block patterns, which are on *Pattern Sheet 1*. Refer to Make the Foundation Patterns on *page 115* to create the foundation patterns.

For blocks, trace:
- 8 *each* of Crow's Foot Block units A and B

From yellow print, cut:
- 1—12⅝" square, cutting it diagonally twice in an X for a total of 4 setting triangles
- 1—8½" square

From black-and-white print, cut:
- 3—2½×42" binding strips

Assemble the Crow's Foot Blocks

Referring to Assemble the Blocks, Crow's Foot Blocks, on *page 115*, foundation-piece a total of two matching Crow's Foot blocks.

Assemble the Quilt Center

1. Referring to the photograph *opposite*, lay out the two blocks, the yellow print 8½" setting square, and the four yellow print setting triangles in diagonal rows.

2. Sew together the pieces in each diagonal row. Press the seam allowances toward the setting triangles.

3. Join the rows to complete the quilt top. Press the seam allowances in one direction.

Complete the Table Runner

1. Layer the quilt top, batting, and backing according to the instructions in Quilter's Schoolhouse, which begins on *page 150*. Quilt as desired.

2. Use the black-and-white print 2½×42" strips to bind the quilt according to the instructions in Quilter's Schoolhouse.

ELEGANT APPLIQUÉ

Appliqué offers endless possibilities. "Poinsettia" is perfect for Christmas, but its patterns can be adapted for year-round use, too. The flower-laden vines of "Twelve Trumpets" can ascend a wall hanging or wreathe a wool table topper. And the appliqués from "Sweet Cherries" will add cheer to your curtains as well as your bed. These natural motifs will have you growing new quilts for years to come.

Poinsettia

The brilliant red poinsettia blossom exudes yuletide cheer throughout the holiday season. An 1880s quiltmaker artfully captured its beauty in this appliqué quilt.

Materials

4⅔ yards of solid cream for appliqué foundations, setting squares, border, and binding

2¼ yards of solid red for border and poinsettia petal, flower, and berry appliqués

2¼ yards of solid green for border, and leaf, poinsettia center, and stem appliqués

⅛ yard of solid gold for berry appliqués

4¼ yards of backing fabric

76×80" of quilt batting

Finished quilt top: 69½×73½"
Finished block: 18" square

Quantities specified for 44/45"-wide, 100% cotton fabrics. All measurements include a ¼" seam allowance. Sew with right sides together unless otherwise stated.

Select the Fabrics

The traditional holiday color trio of red, white, and green in this antique quilt has aged over time to a soft red, cream, and olive green. You can create a similar looking "old" quilt by selecting colors close to those in the photograph *opposite*, then tea-dyeing the finished project. To complete the look, we recommend using an all-cotton batting.

Although there's a slight variation in petal, stem, and leaf placement among the appliqué blocks in this quilt, our pattern shows just one block placement for those elements.

continued

Cut the Fabrics

To make the best use of your fabrics, cut the pieces in the order that follows. Cut the border strips the length of the fabric (parallel to the selvage).

The patterns are on *Pattern Sheet 2*. To make templates of the patterns, follow the instructions in Quilter's Schoolhouse, which begins on *page 150*.

From solid cream, cut:

- 8—2½×42" binding strips
- 2—3×74" border strips
- 2—3×54½" border strips
- 2—2¾×54½" border strips
- 5—20" squares for appliqué foundations
- 4—18½" squares

From solid red, cut:

- 2—3×74" border strips
- 2—3×54½" border strips
- 40 of Pattern A
- 20 of Pattern B
- 80 of Pattern C

From solid green, cut:

- 2—3¼×74" border strips
- 2—3×54½" border strips
- 1—12×42" rectangle, cutting it into twenty ⅞×15" bias strips for stems (For specific instructions, see Cutting Bias Strips in Quilter's Schoolhouse.)
- 20 *each* of patterns D, E, and F
- 5 of Pattern G

From solid gold, cut:

- 80 of Pattern C

Appliqué the Blocks

1. Press the long edges of each solid green ⅞×15" bias strip under ¼" to make stems.

2. Referring to the full-size pattern on *Pattern Sheet 2* for placement, baste four stems onto each of the five solid cream 20"-square appliqué foundations. Then arrange and baste in place the solid red and solid green appliqué shapes.

To reduce bulk, trim the stems where they run under an appliqué piece so that just ¼" remains underneath.

3. Using small slip stitches and threads that match the fabrics, appliqué the shapes to the solid cream foundations to make the blocks. Trim the appliquéd blocks to measure 18½" square, including the seam allowances.

Assemble the Quilt Center

1. Lay out the five appliquéd blocks and the four solid cream 18½" setting squares in three vertical rows. Sew together the blocks in each row. Press the seam allowances in one direction, alternating the direction with the row.

2. Join the rows to make the quilt center. Press the seam allowances in one direction. The pieced quilt center should measure 54½" square, including the seam allowances.

Add the Border

1. Referring to Diagram 1 for placement, sew together a solid cream 2¾x54½" strip, a solid green 3x54½" strip, a solid cream 3x54½" strip, and a solid red 3x54½" strip to make a short border unit. Press the seam allowances in one direction. The border unit should measure 10¼x54½", including the seam allowances. Repeat to make a second short border unit.

2¾x54½"
3x54½"
3x54½"
3x54½"

Diagram 1

2. Sew the short border units to opposite edges of the pieced quilt center along the red strip edges. Press the seam allowances in the same direction as the seam allowances of the border units.

3. Referring to Diagram 2 for placement, sew together a solid green 3¼x74" strip, a solid cream 3x74" strip, and a solid red 3x74" strip to make a long border unit. Press the seam allowances in one direction. The border unit should measure 8¼x74", including the seam allowances. Repeat to make a second long border unit.

3¼x74"
3x74"
3x74"

Diagram 2

4. Sew the long border units to the remaining edges of the pieced quilt center along the red strip edges to complete the quilt top. Press the seam allowances in the same direction as the border unit seam allowances.

Complete the Quilt

1. Layer the quilt top, batting, and backing according to the instructions in Quilter's Schoolhouse, which begins on *page 150*.

2. Quilt as desired. The antique quilt shown was quilted with 3½"-diameter interlocking circles in the setting squares and around the flowers in the appliquéd blocks. The border was quilted with diagonal lines spaced 2" apart and running in both directions.

3. Use the solid cream 2½x42" strips to bind the quilt according to the instructions in Quilter's Schoolhouse.

optional colors

The bright, solid colors that quilt tester Laura Boehnke selected for her wall hanging *below* stand boldly against a solid black background. She finished her project for the holidays by adding a border of gold tartan plaid.

continued

Poinsettia Quilt

optional sizes

If you'd like to make this quilt in a size other than for a throw, use the information *below*.

Alternate quilt sizes	Twin	Full/Queen	King
Number of blocks	6	10	13
Number of blocks wide by long	3×4	4×5	5×5
Number of setting squares	6	10	12
Finished size	73½×87½"	91½×105½"	105½×109½"
Yardage requirements			
Solid cream	5⅞ yards	8⅛ yards	9⅔ yards
Solid red	2¼ yards	2⅔ yards	3¼ yards
Solid green	2¼ yards	2⅔ yards	3¼ yards
Solid gold	⅛ yard	¼ yard	⅓ yard
Backing	5¼ yards	8¼ yards	9⅓ yards
Batting	80×94"	98×112"	112×116"

TABLECLOTH

Dress up a holiday tablecloth with your favorite seasonal appliqués.

Materials

¼ yard of cream print for poinsettia petal appliqués

1 yard total of assorted pink prints for poinsettia petal and poinsettia center appliqués

⅛ yard total of assorted green prints for leaf appliqués

½ yard of dark green print for vine appliqué

Purchased 60×120" tablecloth

Lightweight fusible web

Monofilament thread

Finished tablecloth: 60×120"

Cut the Fabrics

To make the best use of your fabrics, cut the pieces in the order that follows. *Note:* To make this project for an alternate tablecloth size, adjust the length of the appliqué vine and number of flowers and leaves as desired. This project uses "Poinsettia" patterns, which are on *Pattern Sheet 2*.

To use fusible web for appliquéing, as was done in this project, follow these steps.

1. Lay the fusible web, paper side up, over patterns A, E, F, and G. With a pencil, trace the patterns the number of times indicated, leaving ½" between tracings. Cut out each fusible-web shape roughly ¼" outside the traced lines.

2. Following the manufacturer's instructions, press the fusible-web shapes onto the backs of the designated fabrics; let cool. Cut out the fabric shapes on the drawn lines. Peel off the paper backings.

From cream print, cut:
- 20 of Pattern A

From assorted pink prints, cut:
- 20 sets of 5 of Pattern A
- 24 of Pattern G

From assorted green prints, cut:
- 16 *each* of patterns E and F

From dark green print, cut:
- 1—18" square, cutting it into enough ⅞"-wide bias strips to total approximately 340" in length for vine (For specific instructions, see Cutting Bias Strips in Quilter's Schoolhouse, which begins on *page 150*.)

Appliqué the Tablecloth

1. Press the long edges of the dark green print ⅞×340" bias strip under ¼" to make a vine appliqué.

2. Referring to the photograph *opposite* for placement, position the vine appliqué on the tablecloth; baste.

3. Using monofilament thread and a machine zigzag stitch, appliqué the vine in place. Then position and fuse the remaining flower shapes to the tablecloth; appliqué in place to complete the tablecloth.

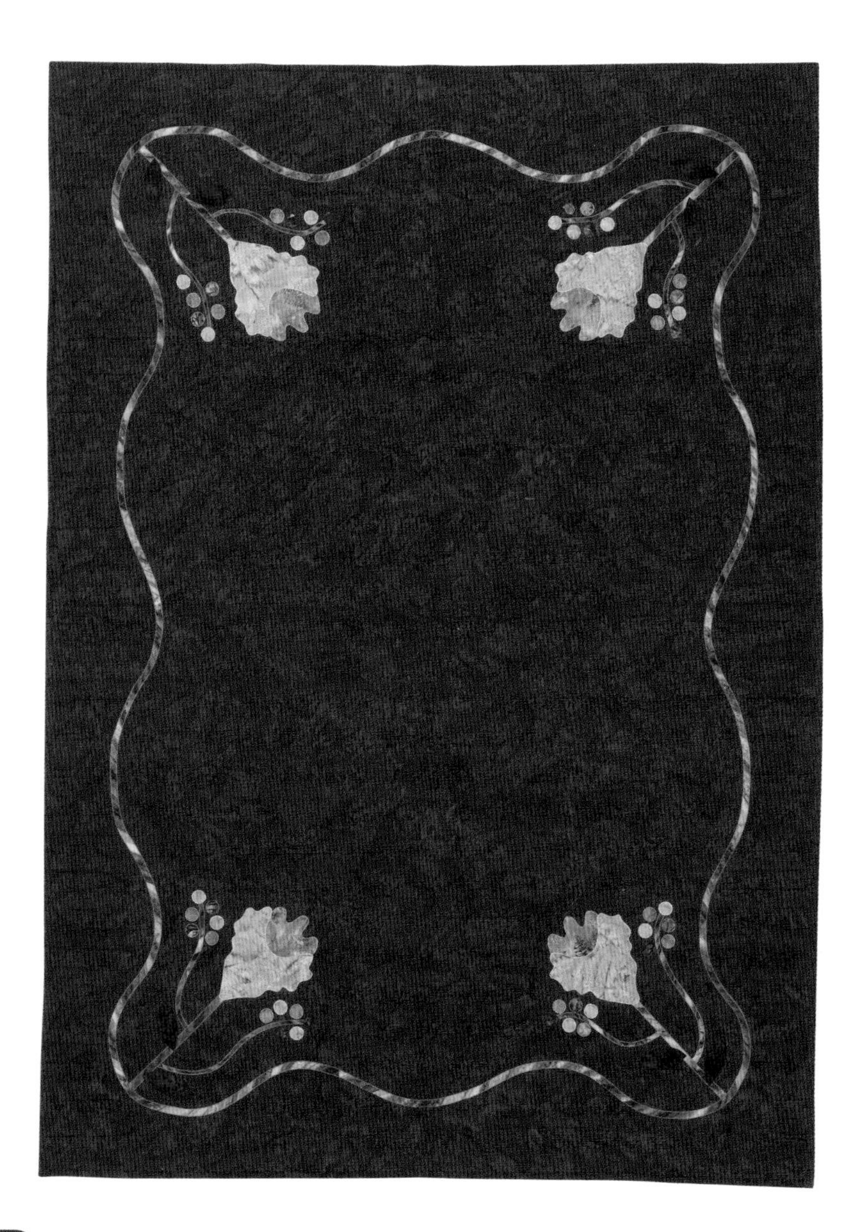

THROW

A brown-and-blue colorway turns this design into a quilt you can use all year.

Materials

2¼ yards of brown print for quilt top and binding

¼ yard of light blue print for flower and berry appliqués

⅛ yard of tan print for flower center and berry appliqués

⅛ yard of dark blue print for leaf appliqués

⅝ yard of blue print for vine, stem, and berry appliqués

2⅔ yards of backing fabric

48×64" of quilt batting

Lightweight fusible web

Finished quilt top: 42×58"

Cut the Fabrics

To make the best use of your fabrics, cut the pieces in the order that follows. This project uses "Poinsettia" patterns, which are on *Pattern Sheet 2*.

To use fusible web for appliquéing, as was done in this project, follow these steps.

1. Lay the fusible web, paper side up, over patterns B, C, D, and F. With a pencil, trace the patterns the number of times indicated, leaving ½" between tracings. Cut out each fusible-web shape roughly ¼" outside the traced lines.

2. Following the manufacturer's instructions, press the fusible-web shapes onto the backs of the designated fabrics; let cool. Cut out the fabric shapes on the drawn lines. Peel off the paper backings.

From brown print, cut:
- 1—42½x58½" rectangle for appliqué foundation
- 6—2½x42" binding strips

From light blue print, cut:
- 4 of Pattern D
- 16 of Pattern C

From tan print, cut:
- 4 of Pattern B
- 16 of Pattern C

From dark blue print, cut:

- 8 of Pattern F

From blue print, cut:

- 1—11×18" rectangle, cutting it into the following bias strips: four ⅞×8" stem appliqués, four ⅝×6½" stem appliqués, and four ⅝×8½" stem appliqués
- 1—16" square, cutting it into enough bias strips to total 180" in length for vine (For specific instructions, see Cutting Bias Strips in Quilter's Schoolhouse, which begins on *page 150.*)
- 16 of Pattern C

Appliqué the Quilt Top

1. Referring to Appliqué the Blocks on *page 124*, Step 1, prepare the blue print continuous vine strip and the blue print stem appliqués.

2. Referring to the photograph *opposite* for placement, position the continuous vine strip and stems on the brown print appliqué foundation.

3. Using matching threads and a machine zigzag stitch, appliqué the vines and stems in place. Then position the flowers, berries, and leaves in place; fuse and appliqué the shapes to the foundation to complete the quilt top.

Complete the Quilt

1. Layer the quilt top, batting, and backing according to the instructions in Quilter's Schoolhouse, which begins on *page 150.* Quilt as desired.

2. Use the brown print 2½×42" strips to bind the quilt according to the instructions in Quilter's Schoolhouse.

TWELVE *Trumpets*

A trumpet vine blooming in her backyard garden prompted quiltmaker Tonee White to produce an uplifting wall hanging using a scrappy mix of homespun plaids, checks, and stripes in a vertical strip design.

Materials

1⅛ yards of tan stripe for appliqué foundations

¾ yard total of assorted light homespun plaids, checks, and stripes for Four-Patch units and flower appliqués

1½ yards total of assorted dark homespun plaids, checks, and stripes for Four-Patch rows and flower appliqués

¼ yard of olive green stripe for vine appliqués

Scraps of green homespun plaids, checks, and stripes for leaf appliqués

⅝ yard of black stripe for border

2⅝ yards of backing fabric

46×60" of quilt batting

Finished quilt top: 39¾×55⅛"

Quantities specified for 44/45"-wide, 100% cotton fabrics. All measurements include a ¼" seam allowance. Sew with right sides together unless otherwise stated.

Cut the Fabrics

To make the best use of your fabrics, cut the pieces in the order that follows. The patterns are on *Pattern Sheet 2.* To make templates of the patterns, follow the instructions in Quilter's Schoolhouse, which begins on *page 150.* Be sure to add a 3⁄16" seam allowance when cutting out appliqué pieces.

continued

From tan stripe, cut:

- 4—8½×42" rectangles

From assorted light homespuns, cut:

- 32—2½" squares
- 2—4½" squares

From assorted dark homespuns, cut:

- 32—2½" squares
- 16—4⅞" squares, cutting each in half diagonally for a total of 32 side triangles
- 2—5¼" squares, cutting each diagonally twice in an X for a total of 8 corner triangles

From remaining assorted light and dark homespuns, cut:

- 12 *each* of patterns A, B, C, and E
- 6 of Pattern D
- 1 of Pattern F
- 39 of Pattern G

From olive green stripe, cut:

- 1—9×42" rectangle, cutting it into enough ⅞"-wide bias strips to total 200" in length for vines (For specific instructions, see Cutting Bias Strips in Quilter's Schoolhouse.)

From green homespun scraps, cut:

- 5 of Pattern H
- 8 of Pattern I
- 2 *each* of patterns H reversed, J, and L
- 5 *each* of patterns K and M
- 3 of Pattern N

From black stripe, cut:

- 5—3×42" strips for border

Assemble the Four-Patch Rows

1. Referring to Diagram 1 for placement, sew together two light homespun 2½" squares and two dark homespun 2½" squares in pairs. Press the seam allowances in opposite directions. Then join the pairs to make a Four-Patch unit. Press the seam allowance in one direction. The pieced Four-Patch unit should measure 4½" square, including the seam allowances. Repeat to make a total of 16 Four-Patch units.

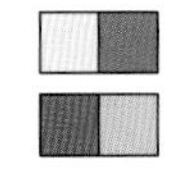

Diagram 1

2. Sew a pair of dark homespun side triangles to opposite edges of a Four-Patch unit to make a unit 1 (see Diagram 2). Press the seam allowances toward the triangles. Repeat with 12 additional Four-Patch units and one light homespun 4½" square to make a total of 14 of unit 1.

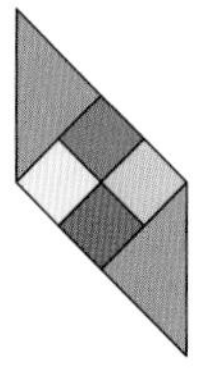

Diagram 2

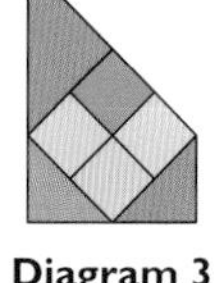

Diagram 3

3. Referring to Diagram 3, join a dark homespun side triangle and a dark homespun corner triangle to opposite edges of a remaining Four-Patch unit. Press the seam allowances toward the triangles. Add a dark homespun corner triangle to make a unit 2. Press the seam allowances toward the triangles. Repeat with the remaining Four-Patch units and remaining light homespun 4½" square to make a total of four of unit 2.

4. Referring to the photograph *opposite* and Diagram 4 for placement, lay out seven of unit 1 and two of unit 2; sew together, carefully matching seams, to make a pieced Four-Patch row. Press the seam allowances in one direction. The pieced row should measure 6⅛×51⅛", including the seam allowances. Repeat to make a second pieced Four-Patch row.

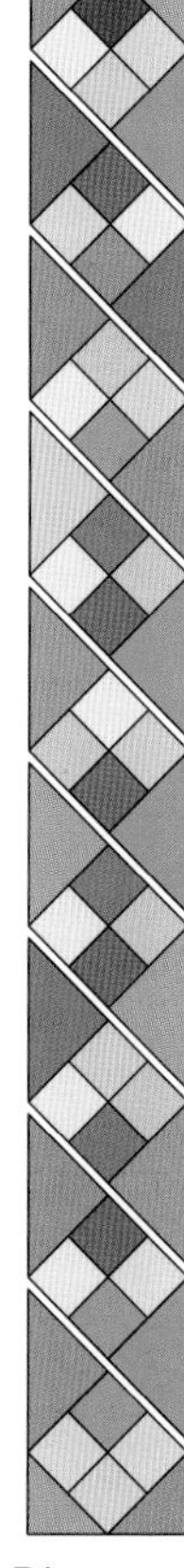

Diagram 4

Assemble the Quilt Center

1. Cut and piece the tan stripe 8½×42" rectangles to make the following:
   - 3—8½×51⅛" rectangles for appliqué foundations

2. Referring to the photograph *opposite*, lay out the Four-Patch rows and the tan stripe appliqué foundations; sew together to make the quilt center. Press the seam allowances toward the tan stripe appliqué foundations. The pieced quilt center should measure 35¾×51⅛", including the seam allowances.

continued

Add the Border

1. Cut and piece the black stripe 3×42" strips to make the following:
- 2—3×57" border strips
- 2—3×42" border strips

2. With midpoints aligned, pin the black stripe long border strips to the long edges and the black stripe short border strips to the short edges of the pieced quilt center; allow excess border fabric to extend beyond the corners. Sew each border strip to the quilt center, beginning and ending the seams ¼" from the corners. Press the seam allowances toward the border.

3. Miter the border corners to complete the quilt top. For information on mitering corners, see Quilter's Schoolhouse, which begins on *page 150.*

Appliqué the Foundations

1. Referring to the photograph on *page 133* for placement, arrange the olive green stripe bias strips as vines atop the tan stripe appliqué foundations. Then arrange the flower, leaf, and circle appliqué pieces along the vines and in one block in each of the pieced Four-Patch rows. Some motifs will lie under vines and others will be on top. Baste the appliqué shapes in place.

2. Using cream linen thread and a straight stitch, hand-appliqué the pieces in place. (Designer Tonee White brings her needle up at the outside edge of the motif and pushes it back down ⅛" to ⅜" in from the motif's edge.)

Complete the Quilt

1. Layer the quilt top, batting, and backing according to the instructions in Quilter's Schoolhouse, which begins on *page 150.*

2. Quilt as desired. Tonee machine-quilted around each leaf and flower, stitching ¼" outside the edges, and machine-quilted a crosshatch pattern through the quilt center. She hand-stitched an X through each Four-Patch unit and hand-quilted ¼" from the edge of each triangle in the Four-Patch rows.

3. Trim the batting and backing so all edges are ¼" smaller than the quilt top.

4. Fold the quilt top border around to the backing, covering the raw edges of the batting and backing. Hand-stitch in place, mitering the corners.

optional colors

Quilt tester Laura Boehnke cut her setting triangles out of a single plaid but maintained a scrappy look in her Four-Patch units and flower appliqués. These soft, muted pastels offer a gentle variation on the original homespun quilt.

WOOL PENNY RUG

Trumpet flowers and a scalloped border twist around this appliquéd wool table topper.

Materials

30" square of blue plaid felted wool for appliqué foundation

2—33" squares of solid black felted wool for backing

Scraps of assorted maroon, blue, and tan felted wool for flower appliqués

Scrap of yellow felted wool for flower appliqués

Scrap of green plaid felted wool for leaf appliqués

7×9" piece of green felted wool for leaf and vine appliqués

Perle cotton No. 5: black, gold, and green

15 black glass beads

Finished penny rug: 33" diameter

continued

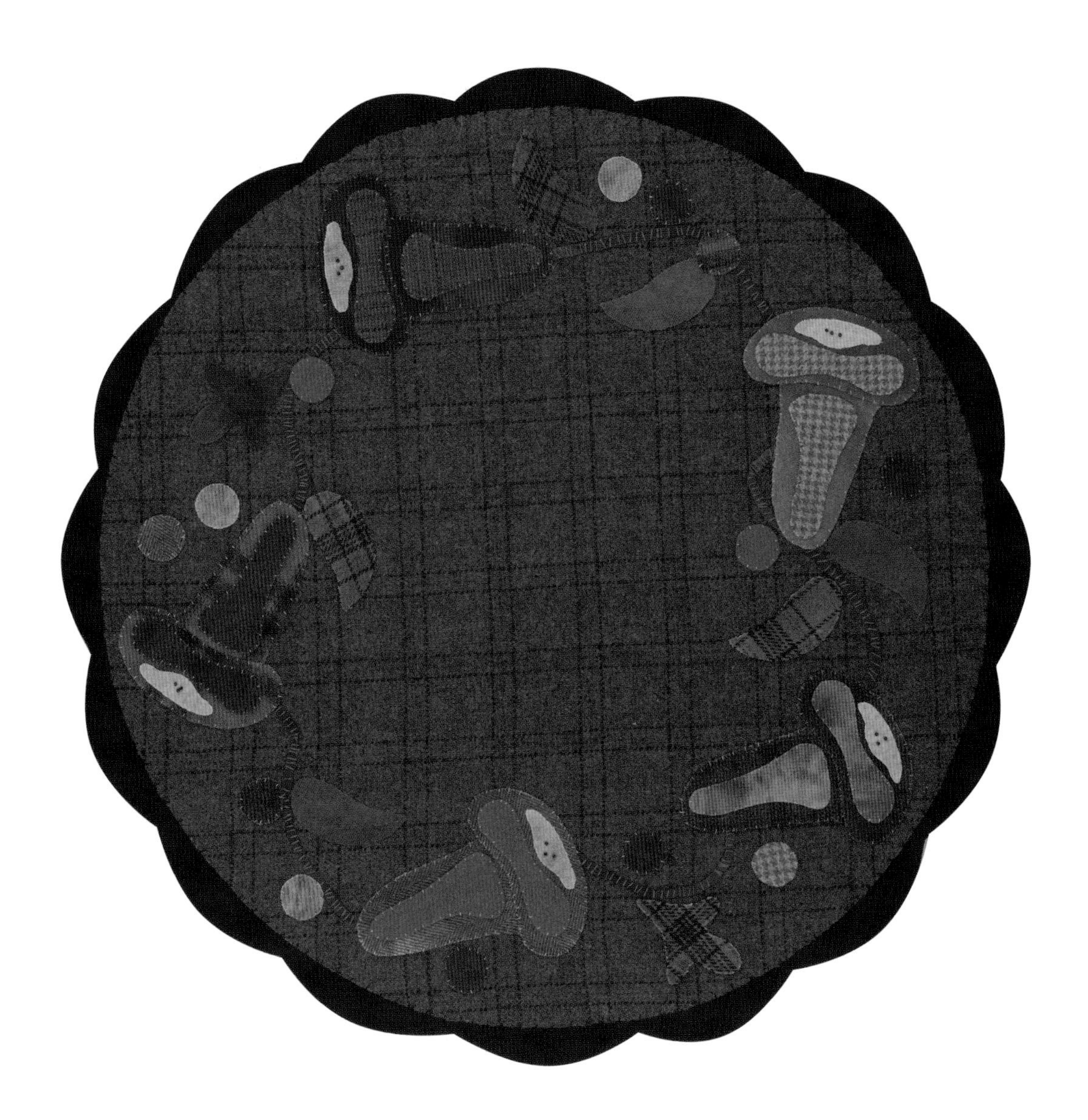

Cut the Fabrics

To make the best use of your fabrics, cut the pieces in the order that follows. This project uses "Twelve Trumpets" appliqué patterns, which are on *Pattern Sheet 2*. To make templates of the patterns, follow the instructions in Quilter's Schoolhouse, which begins on *page 150*. It is not necessary to add seam allowances to the wool appliqué shapes. The patterns for the appliqué foundation circle and the scalloped backing circles are on *Pattern Sheet 1*.

From blue plaid wool, cut:
- 1 of Circle Pattern

From solid black wool, cut:
- 2 of Scallop Pattern

From assorted maroon, blue, and tan wool, cut:
- 5 *each* of patterns A, C, D, and E
- 13 of Pattern G

From yellow wool, cut:
- 5 of Pattern B

From green plaid wool, cut:
- 3 of Pattern H
- 1 of Pattern M

From green wool, cut:
- 5—¼×9" bias strips for vine appliqués (For specific instructions, see Cutting Bias Strips in Quilter's Schoolhouse.)
- 2 of Pattern H
- 1 of Pattern H reversed
- 1 of Pattern M

Appliqué the Foundation

1. Referring to the Appliqué Placement Diagram, position the flower, leaf, and vine appliqués atop the blue plaid foundation circle. Then remove all the pieces except the vines; baste them in place.

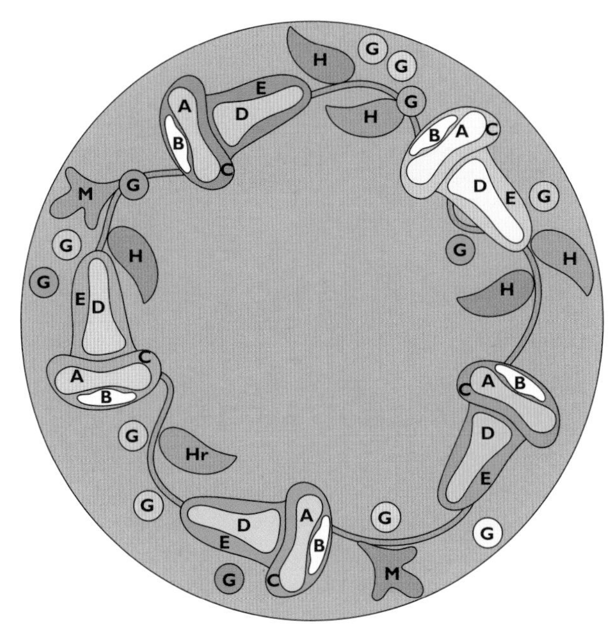

Appliqué Placement Diagram

2. Use green perle cotton to couch the vines with small stitches ¼" to ⅜" apart (see diagram *below*).

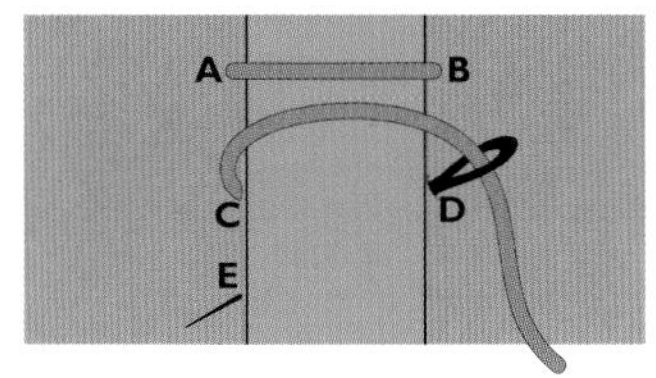

Couching Stitch

3. Replace the remaining appliqué shapes; baste them in place. Use a running stitch ⅛" inside the leaf edges to appliqué the leaves to the foundation.

To make a running stitch, work with a length of green perle cotton no longer than 18". Insert your needle into the wrong side of the appliqué foundation directly beneath the edge of the appliqué piece. Bring your needle up through the appliqué piece about ⅛" from the edge (see diagram *below*).

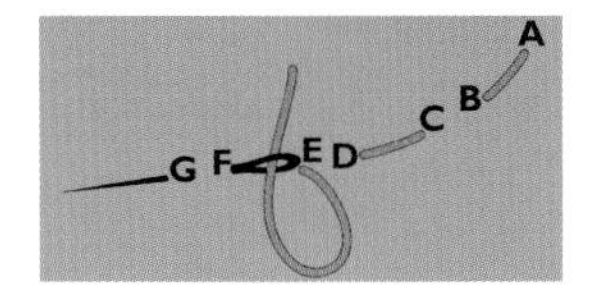

Running Stitch

Rock the needle in and out through both the appliqué piece and the foundation, staying about ⅛" inside the appliqué edge and taking small, evenly spaced stitches. Continue in this manner to secure the leaves to the foundation. Do a running stitch down the center of the H leaves.

4. Tack-stitch the remaining appliqué pieces using gold perle cotton.

To tack-stitch, pull your needle up at A (see diagram *below*) and push it down at B. Come up at C and go down at D, continuing in the same manner around the entire shape.

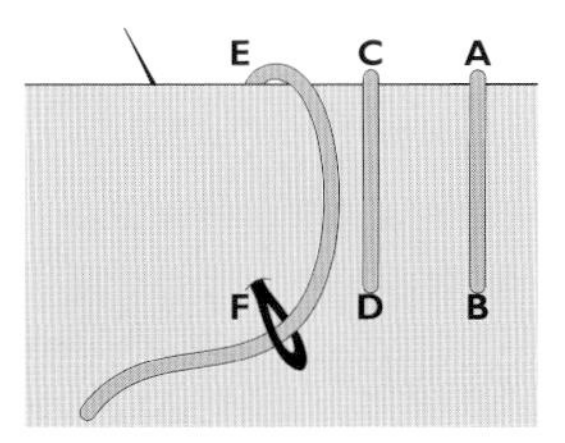

Tack Stitch

5. Continue working from the bottom layer to the top layer until all appliqués have been stitched to the foundation. Using black perle cotton, attach three glass beads to each yellow B flower piece.

Complete the Penny Rug

1. Center the appliquéd blue plaid circle on a solid black scalloped circle; use the black perle cotton to tack-stitch it in place.

2. With wrong sides together, layer the appliquéd solid black scalloped circle with the remaining solid black scalloped circle.

3. Using black perle cotton, blanket-stitch around the edges of the black circles.

To blanket-stitch, pull your needle up at A (see diagram *below*), form a reverse L shape with the thread, and hold the angle of the L shape in place with your thumb. Push your needle down at B and come up at C to secure the stitch.

At the end, run your thread under the first stitches and secure it to complete the penny rug.

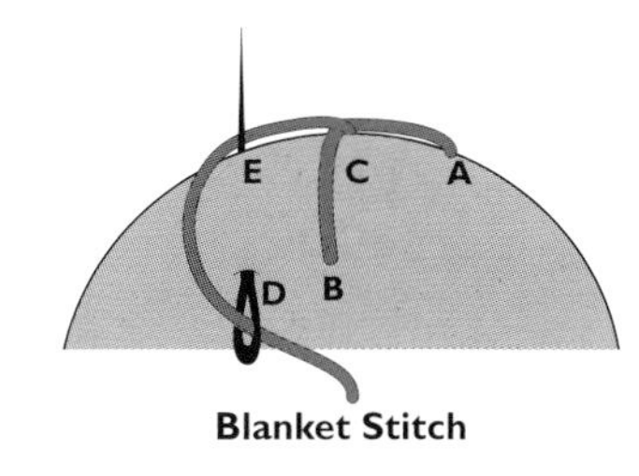

Blanket Stitch

BED QUILT

Select lively prints for the setting strips and you can forgo the muted-color appliqués of the original project.

Materials

2⅔ yards total of assorted pastel prints for Four-Patch units

2½ yards total of assorted solid pastels for Four-Patch rows

3 yards *each* of pink, blue, yellow, and lavender florals for panels

⅞ yard of bright pink print for binding

7⅞ yards of backing fabric

96×108" of quilt batting

Finished quilt top: 90⅝×101¾"

Cut the Fabrics

To make the best use of your fabrics, cut the pieces in the order that follows. Cut the floral panels lengthwise (parallel to the selvage).

From assorted pastel prints, cut:

- 252 sets of 2—2½" squares

From assorted solid pastels, cut:

- 56—6⅞" squares, cutting each diagonally twice in an X for a total of 224 side triangles
- 14—3¾" squares, cutting each in half diagonally for a total of 28 corner triangles

From *each* pink floral and *each* blue floral, cut:

- 2—8½×101¾" panels

From *each* yellow floral and *each* lavender floral, cut:

- 1—8½×101¾" panel

From bright pink print, cut:

- 10—2½×42" binding strips

Assemble the Four-Patch Rows

Referring to Assemble the Four-Patch Rows on *page 132* and the photograph *opposite* for placement, make seven pieced Four-Patch rows. Start by using the sets of pastel print 2½" squares to make 126 Four-Patch units. Then add the solid pastel side and corner triangles to make 112 of unit 1 and 14 of unit 2.

Assemble the Quilt Top

1. Referring to the photograph *opposite*, alternate the Four-Patch rows with the six pink, blue, lavender, and yellow floral 8½×101¾" panels.

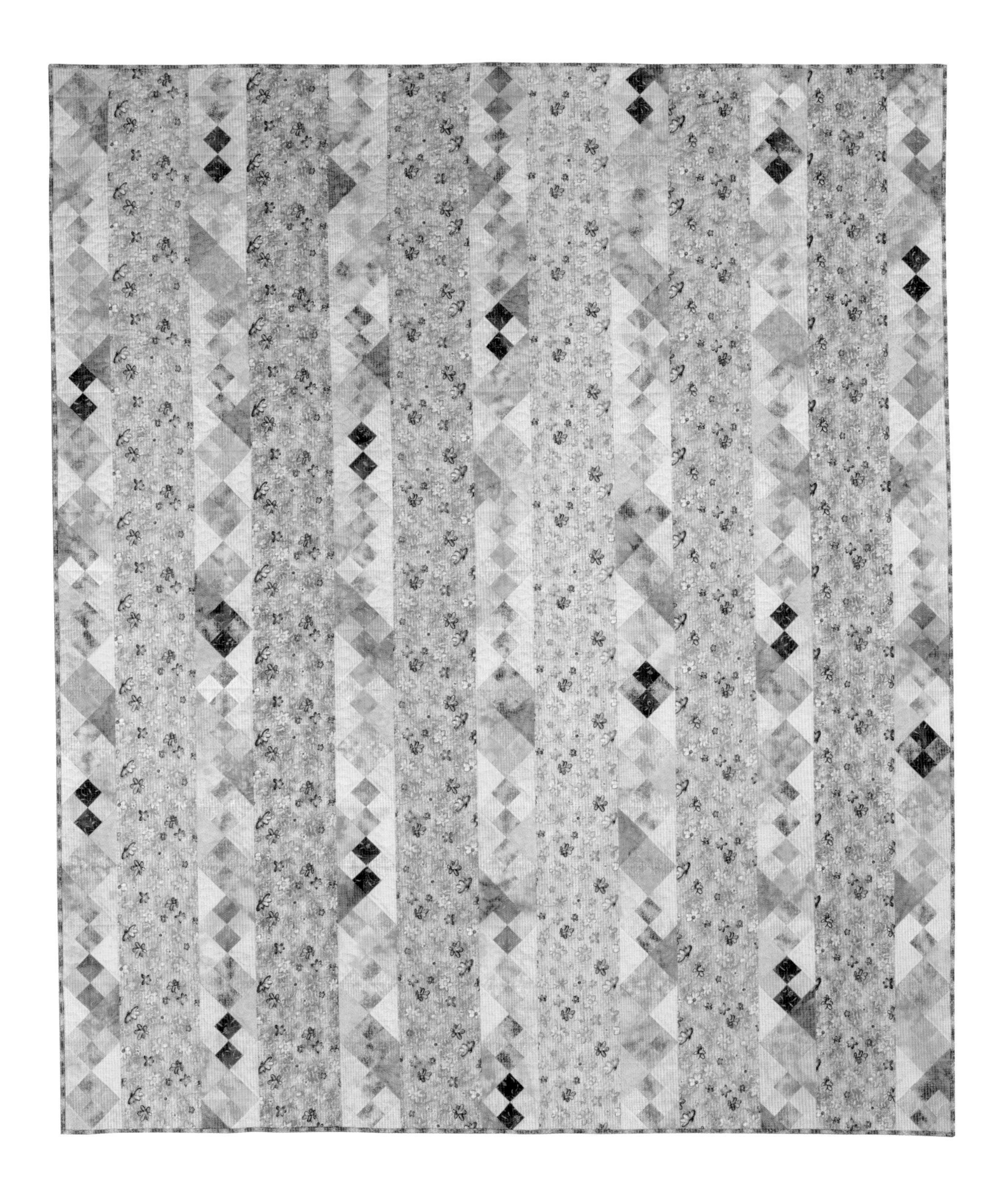

2. Sew together the rows and panels to make the quilt top. Press the seam allowances toward the floral panels.

Complete the Quilt

1. Layer the quilt top, batting, and backing according to the instructions in Quilter's Schoolhouse, which begins on *page 150*.
2. Quilt as desired. Sue Urich machine-quilted an X through each Four-Patch square, a partial flower in the side and corner triangles, and loose stippling through the floral panels.
3. Use the bright pink print 2½×42" strips to bind the quilt according to the instructions in Quilter's Schoolhouse.

SWEET *Cherries*

Designers Janey Edwards and Roxie Wood found inspiration for this quilt in an elegant Japanese fabric with a cherry motif. They decided a traditional Basket block would showcase the print beautifully.

Materials

12—4×12" pieces of assorted brown, green, red, and purple prints for basket handle appliqués and basket base triangles

6—18×22" pieces (fat quarters) of assorted beige prints for block backgrounds

5/8 yard of cherry print for baskets

7/8 yard of brown print for sawtooth borders

1 1/8 yards of red tone-on-tone print for sawtooth borders and inner border

2 yards of tan-and-white print for setting squares, setting triangles, and corner triangles

2 3/8 yards of light tan print for outer border

2/3 yard of brown tone-on-tone print for vine appliqués

5—1/8-yard pieces of assorted green prints for leaf appliqués

Scraps of red and purple prints for cherry appliqués

2/3 yard of dark tan print for binding

5 1/4 yards of backing fabric

76×93" of quilt batting

Finished quilt top: 69 1/4×87"
Finished block: 10" square

Quantities specified for 44/45"-wide, 100% cotton fabrics. All measurements include a 1/4" seam allowance. Sew with right sides together unless otherwise stated.

continued

Cut the Fabrics

To make the best use of your fabrics, cut the pieces in the order that follows. The setting and corner triangles are cut slightly larger than necessary. You'll trim them to the correct size once you've pieced your quilt center.

The patterns are on *Pattern Sheet 2.* To make templates of the patterns, follow the instructions in Quilter's Schoolhouse, which begins on *page 150.*

From *each* assorted brown, green, red, and purple prints, cut:

- 1—3⅜" squares, cutting each in half diagonally for a total of 2 small triangles
- 1 of Pattern A

From *each* assorted beige prints, cut:

- 1—8⅜" squares, cutting each in half diagonally for a total of 2 large triangles
- 1—5⅞" squares, cutting each in half diagonally for a total of 2 medium triangles
- 4—3×5½" rectangles

From cherry print, cut:

- 6—8⅜" squares, cutting each in half diagonally for a total of 12 large triangles

From brown print, cut:

- 192—2⅛" squares, cutting each in half diagonally for a total of 384 sawtooth triangles
- 48—1¾" squares

From red tone-on-tone print, cut:

- 7—1½×42" strips for inner border
- 192—2⅛" squares, cutting each in half diagonally for a total of 384 sawtooth triangles

From tan-and-white print, cut:

- 3—19½" squares, cutting each diagonally twice in an X for a total of 12 setting triangles (you'll have 2 leftover triangles)
- 6—13" squares
- 2—10" squares, cutting each in half diagonally for a total of 4 corner triangles

From light tan print, cut:

- 10—7½×42" strips for outer border

From brown tone-on-tone print, cut:

- 1—22×42" rectangle, cutting it into enough 1½"-wide bias strips to total approximately 530" in length for vines (For specific instructions, see Cutting Bias Strips in Quilter's Schoolhouse.)

From assorted green prints, cut:

- 60 *each* of patterns B and C

From assorted red and purple print scraps, cut:

- 80 of Pattern D

From dark tan print, cut:

- 8—2½×42" binding strips

Assemble the Basket Blocks

1. Prepare the assorted print A basket handles for appliqué by finger-pressing under the $\frac{3}{16}$" seam allowances.

2. Referring to Diagram 1 for placement, baste a basket handle to a beige print large triangle. Using small slip stitches and thread that matches the fabric, appliqué the basket handle in place.

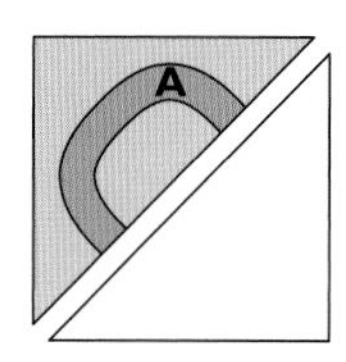

Diagram 1

3. Sew together the appliquéd triangle and a cherry print large triangle to make a large triangle-square (see Diagram 1). Press the seam allowance toward the cherry print triangle. The pieced triangle-square should measure 8" square, including the seam allowances.

4. Referring to Diagram 2, join a beige print 3×5½" rectangle and an assorted print small triangle to make a basket base unit. Press the seam allowance toward the tan print rectangle. Make a second basket base unit that is a mirror image of the first.

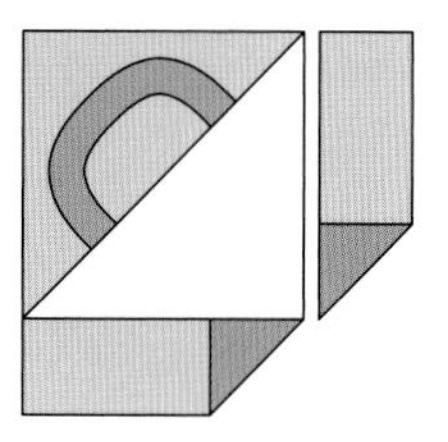
Diagram 2

5. Sew the basket base units to the large triangle-square (see Diagram 2). Press all seam allowances toward the triangle-square.

6. Referring to Diagram 3, join a tan print medium triangle to the diagonal edge of the Step 5 pieced unit to complete the Basket block. The pieced Basket block should measure 10½" square, including the seam allowances.

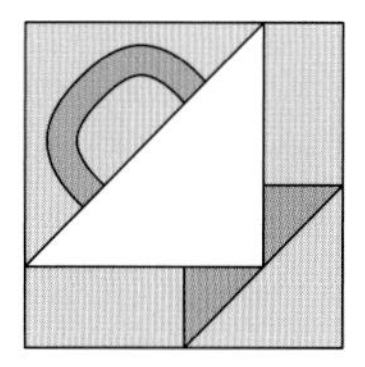
Diagram 3

7. Repeat steps 2 through 6 to make a total of 12 Basket blocks.

Add the Sawtooth Borders

1. Sew together one red tone-on-tone print sawtooth triangle and one brown print sawtooth triangle to make a triangle-square. Press the seam allowance toward the brown print triangle. The pieced triangle-square should measure 1¾" square, including the seam allowances. Repeat to make a total of 32 triangle-squares.

2. Referring to Diagram 4, sew together eight triangle-squares in a row to make a sawtooth border strip. Press the seam allowances away from the center of the strip. Repeat to make a total of four sawtooth border strips.

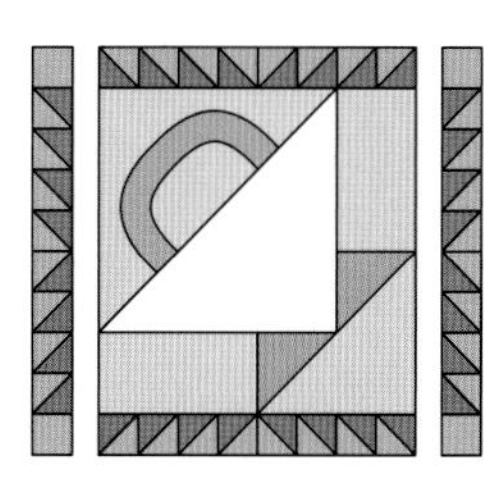
Diagram 4

3. Sew sawtooth border strips to opposite edges of a Basket block. Press the seam allowances toward the Basket block.

4. Add a brown print 1¾" square to each end of the remaining sawtooth border strips. Press the seam allowances toward the brown print squares. Join the sawtooth border strips to the remaining edges of the Basket block. Press the seam allowances toward the block. The Basket block now should measure 13" square, including the seam allowances.

5. Repeat steps 1 through 4 to add sawtooth borders to all 12 Basket blocks.

Assemble the Quilt Center

1. Referring to the Quilt Assembly Diagram for placement, lay out the 12 Basket blocks, the six tan-and-white print 13" setting squares, 10 tan-and-white print setting triangles, and the four tan-and-white print corner triangles in diagonal rows.

Quilt Assembly Diagram

2. Sew together the pieces in each diagonal row. Press the seam allowances toward the setting squares and triangles. Then join the rows. Press the seam allowances in one direction. Add the remaining two corner triangles to complete the quilt center.

3. Trim the quilt center, leaving a ¼" seam allowance beyond the Basket block corners (see Diagram 5), to measure 53¾×71½", including the seam allowances. Double-check the corners to make sure they are 90° angles, trim if necessary.

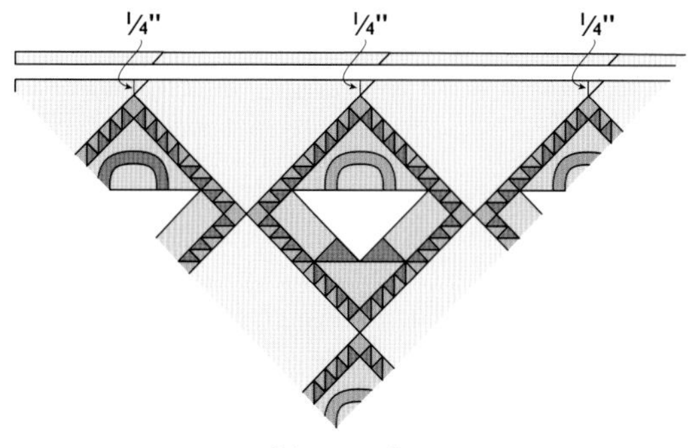

Diagram 5

continued

Add the Borders

1. Cut and piece the red tone-on-tone print 1½x42" strips to make the following:
- 2—1½x75½" inner border strips
- 2—1½x57¾" inner border strips

2. Cut and piece the light tan print 7½x42" strips to make the following:
- 2—7½x89½" outer border strips
- 2—7½x71¾" outer border strips

3. Aligning the centers, pair the red print inner border strips with the tan print outer border strips according to length. Join the long edges to make a total of four border units. Press the seam allowances toward the red print strips.

4. Add the border units to the quilt center with mitered corners to complete the quilt top. For specific instructions on mitering corners, see Quilter's Schoolhouse, which begins on *page 150.*

Appliqué the Outer Border

1. Piece the brown tone-on-tone print 1½"-wide bias strips to make one 530"-long strip. Fold the strip in half lengthwise with the wrong side inside; press. Stitch ¼" from the long edges, then trim the seam allowances to ⅛". Refold the strip, centering the seam in the back; press.

2. Cut the brown tone-on-tone print 530"-long strip into the following:
- 4—72"-long vine appliqués
- 40—3½"-long stem appliqués
- 28—2½"-long stem appliqués

3. Prepare the green print B and C leaf appliqué pieces and the red and purple D cherry appliqué pieces by finger-pressing under the 3/16" seam allowances along edges that will be exposed; you do not need to turn under edges that will be overlapped by other pieces.

4. Referring to the Border Appliqué Diagram, which shows one-quarter of the border, and the photograph *opposite,* lay out the appliqué pieces on the light tan print outer border. Baste, beginning with the pieces on the bottom and working up.

Border Appliqué Diagram

5. Using small slip stitches and threads that match the fabrics, appliqué the pieces to the border.

Complete the Quilt

1. Layer the appliquéd quilt top, batting, and backing according to the instructions in Quilter's Schoolhouse, which begins on *page 150.* Quilt as desired.

2. Use the dark tan print 2½x42" strips to bind the quilt according to the instructions in Quilter's Schoolhouse.

optional colors

Floral prints in the baskets and outer border serve as quilt tester Laura Boehnke's focal point in her version of this project. Instead of using appliqué, Laura dressed up this quilt with a pieced inner border that matches her baskets' handles and bases.

CURTAINS

A vine appliqué gracefully climbs up the edge of these loose-woven linen curtains.

Materials

½ yard of brown print for vine and stem appliqués

Scraps of assorted brown and green prints for leaf appliqués

Scraps of gold prints for cherry appliqués

Purchased 82½"-long green linen curtain panels

½ yard of lightweight fusible web

Finished appliqué: 7×82½"

Cut the Fabrics

To make the best use of your fabrics, cut the pieces in the order that follows. This project uses "Sweet Cherries" patterns B, C, and D on *Pattern Sheet 2*. To make templates of the patterns, follow the instructions in Quilter's Schoolhouse, which begins on *page 150*.

To use fusible web for appliquéing, as was done in this project, complete the following steps.

1. Lay the fusible web, paper side up, over the patterns. With a pencil, trace each pattern the number of times indicated, leaving ½" between tracings. Cut out the fusible-web shapes roughly ¼" outside the traced lines.

2. Following the manufacturer's instructions, press the fusible-web shapes onto the backs of the designated fabrics; let cool. Cut out the fabric shapes on the drawn lines. Peel off the paper backings.

From brown print, cut:

- 1—18" square, cutting it into enough 1½"-wide bias strips to total approximately 180" in length for vines (For specific instructions, see Cutting Bias Strips in Quilter's Schoolhouse.)
- 5—1×20" strips for stem appliqués

From green and brown print scraps, cut:

- 22 *each* of patterns B and C

From gold print scraps, cut:

- 22 of Pattern D

Appliqué the Curtains

1. Referring to Appliqué the Outer Border on *page 145*, Step 1, use the brown print 1½"-wide bias strips to make two 90"-long vines. Repeat with the brown print 1×20" strips and cut them into forty-four 2"-long stems.

2. Referring to Appliqué the Outer Border, Step 4, on *page 145*, and the photograph *above left*, arrange one 90"-long vine along one long edge of a curtain panel; baste. Arrange twenty-two 2"-long stems along the vine, each with one end underneath the vine; baste. Arrange and fuse 11 brown and green print B leaf pieces, 11 brown and green print C leaf pieces, and 11 gold print D cherry pieces in place; let the fabrics cool. Using matching thread, machine-satin-stitch all appliqué edges. Repeat to appliqué the second curtain panel.

BED QUILT

A basket-weave print fabric adds texture to the blocks and borders in this elegant bed quilt.

Materials

1⅛ yards of black leaf print for basket handle appliqués and basket base triangles

1¼ yards of black toile for block backgrounds

1¾ yards of gold print for block backgrounds

2⅜ yards of basket-weave print for baskets, inner border, and piping

8¼ yards of black-and-gold floral for setting squares, setting triangles, corner triangles, outer border, and binding

9⅓ yards of backing fabric

112" square of quilt batting

Finished quilt top: 106" square

continued

Cut the Fabrics

To make the best use of your fabrics, cut the pieces in the order that follows. The setting and corner triangles are cut slightly larger than necessary. You'll trim them to the correct size once you've pieced your quilt center. Cut the outer border strips lengthwise (parallel to the selvage).

This project uses "Sweet Cherries" Pattern A on *Pattern Sheet 2*. To make a template of the pattern, follow the instructions in Quilter's Schoolhouse, which begins on *page 150*.

From black leaf print, cut:

- 36—3⅜" squares, cutting each in half diagonally for a total of 72 small triangles
- 36 of Pattern A

From black toile, cut:

- 18—8⅜" squares, cutting each in half diagonally for a total of 36 large triangles

From gold print, cut:

- 18—5⅞" squares, cutting each in half diagonally for a total of 36 medium triangles
- 72—3×5½" rectangles

From basket-weave print, cut:

- 9—2½×42" strips for inner border
- 11—1×42" strips for piping
- 18—8⅜" squares, cutting each in half diagonally for a total of 36 large triangles

From black-and-gold floral, cut:

- 2—8×106½" outer border strips
- 2—8×91½" outer border strips
- 11—2½×42" strips for binding
- 5—17½" squares, cutting each diagonally twice in an X for a total of 20 setting triangles
- 25—10½" squares
- 2—9⅛" squares, cutting each in half diagonally for a total of 4 corner triangles

Assemble the Basket Blocks

Referring to the photograph *opposite* and Assemble the Basket Blocks on *page 142*, use the black leaf print Pattern A handles and small triangles, the black toile large triangles, the gold print medium triangles and 3×5½" rectangles, and the basket-weave print large triangles to make 36 Basket blocks.

Assemble the Quilt Center

1. Referring to the photograph *opposite*, lay out the 36 Basket blocks, the 25 black-and-gold floral 10½" setting squares, 20 black-and-gold floral setting triangles, and the four black-and-gold floral corner triangles in 11 diagonal rows.

2. Sew together the pieces in each diagonal row. Press the seam allowances toward the setting squares and triangles. Then join the rows. Press the seam allowances in one direction. Add the remaining two corner triangles to complete the quilt center.

3. Trim the quilt center, leaving 1" beyond the Basket block corners (see Diagram 5 on *page 143*), to measure 87½" square, including the seam allowances. Double-check the corners to make sure they are 90° angles; trim if necessary.

Add the Borders

1. Cut and piece the basket-weave print 2½×42" strips to make the following:
   - 2—2½×91½" inner border strips
   - 2—2½×87½" inner border strips

2. Sew the short basket-weave print inner border strips to opposite edges of the quilt center. Add the long basket-weave print inner border strips to the remaining edges of the quilt center. Press the seam allowances toward the inner border.

3. Sew the black-and-gold floral 8×91½" outer border strips to opposite edges of the quilt center. Add the black-and-gold floral 8×106½" outer border strips to the remaining edges of the quilt center to complete the quilt top. Press the seam allowances toward the outer border.

Complete the Quilt

1. Layer the quilt top, batting, and backing according to the instructions in Quilter's Schoolhouse, which begins on *page 150*. Quilt as desired.

2. Cut and piece the basket-weave print 1×42" strips to make a 434"-long piping strip.

3. With the wrong side inside, fold and press the basket-weave print strip in half lengthwise to make a ½"-wide piping strip. Aligning raw edges

and using a ¼" seam, baste the piping strip to the quilt top, mitering the corners.

4. Use the black-and-gold floral 2½×42" strips to bind the quilt according to the instructions in Quilter's Schoolhouse. *Note:* About ⅛" of the basket-weave piping will show between the quilt top and the binding edge once the binding is turned to the back.

QUILTER'S SCHOOLHOUSE

GETTING STARTED

Before you begin any project, collect the tools and materials you'll need in one place.

Tools

CUTTING

Acrylic ruler: To aid in making perfectly straight cuts with a rotary cutter, choose a ruler of thick, clear plastic. Many sizes are available. A 6×24" ruler marked in ¼" increments with 30°, 45°, and 60° angles is a good first purchase.

Rotary-cutting mat: A rotary cutter should always be used with a mat designed specifically for it. In addition to protecting the table, the mat helps keep the fabric from shifting while you cut. Often these mats are described as self-healing, meaning the blade does not leave slash marks or grooves in the surface, even after repeated usage. While many shapes and styles are available, a 16×23" mat marked with a 1" grid, with hash marks at ⅛" increments and 45° and 60° angles is a good choice.

Rotary cutter: The round blade of a rotary cutter will cut up to six layers of fabric at once. Because the blade is so sharp, be sure to purchase one with a safety guard and keep the guard over the blade when you're not cutting. The blade can be removed from the handle and replaced when it gets dull. Commonly available in three sizes, a good first blade is a 45 mm.

Scissors: You'll need one pair for cutting fabric and another for cutting paper and plastic.

Pencils and other marking tools: Marks made with special quilt markers are easy to remove after sewing.

Template plastic: This slightly frosted plastic comes in sheets about 1⁄16" thick.

PIECING

Iron and ironing board

Sewing thread: Use 100-percent-cotton thread.

Sewing machine: Any machine in good working order with well-adjusted tension will produce pucker-free patchwork seams.

APPLIQUÉ

Fusible web: Instead of the traditional method, secure cutout shapes to the background of an appliqué block with this iron-on adhesive.

Hand-sewing needles: For hand appliqué, most quilters like fine quilting needles.

HAND QUILTING

Frame or hoop: You'll get smaller, more even stitches if you stretch your quilt as you stitch. A frame supports the quilt's weight, ensures even tension, and frees both your hands for stitching. However, once set up, it cannot be disassembled until the quilting is complete. Quilting hoops are more portable and less expensive.

Quilting needles: A "between" or quilting needle is short with a small eye. Common sizes are 8, 9, and 10; size 8 is best for beginners.

Quilting thread: Quilting thread is stronger than sewing thread.

Thimble: This finger cover relieves the pressure required to push a needle through several layers of fabric and batting.

Basic Tools
1. Rotary-cutting mat
2. Template plastic
3. Template
4. Acrylic rulers
5. Chalk marker
6. Marking pencil
7. Water-erasable marker
8. Rotary cutter
9. Bias bars
10. Quilting stencils

MACHINE QUILTING

Darning foot: You may find this tool, also called a hopper foot, in your sewing machine's accessory kit. If not, have the model and brand of your machine available when you go to purchase one. It is used for free-motion stitching.

Safety pins: They hold the layers together during quilting.

Table: Use a large work surface that's level with your machine bed.

Thread: Use 100-percent-cotton quilting thread, cotton-wrapped polyester quilting thread, or fine nylon monofilament thread.

Walking foot: This sewing-machine accessory helps you keep long, straight quilting lines smooth and pucker-free.

Choose Your Fabrics

It is no surprise that most quilters prefer 100-percent-cotton fabrics for quiltmaking. Cotton fabric minimizes seam distortion, presses crisply, and is easy to quilt. Most patterns, including those in this book, specify quantities for 44/45"-wide fabrics unless otherwise noted. Our projects call for a little extra yardage in length to allow for minor errors and slight shrinkage.

Prepare Your Fabrics

There are conflicting opinions about the need to prewash fabric. The debate is a modern one because most antique quilts were made with unwashed fabric. However, the dyes and sizing used today are unlike those used a century ago.

Prewashing fabric offers quilters certainty as its main advantage. Today's fabrics resist bleeding and shrinkage, but some of both can occur in some fabrics—an unpleasant prospect once you've assembled a quilt. Some quilters find prewashed fabric easier to quilt. If you choose to prewash your fabric, press it well before cutting.

Other quilters prefer the crispness of unwashed fabric, especially for machine piecing. And, if you use fabrics with the same fiber content throughout a quilt, then any shrinkage that occurs in its first washing should be uniform. Some quilters find this small amount of shrinkage desirable, since it gives a quilt a slightly puckered, antique look.

We recommend you prewash a scrap of each fabric to test it for shrinkage and bleeding. If you choose to prewash an entire fabric piece, unfold it to a single layer. Wash it in warm water, which will allow the fabric to shrink and/or bleed. If the fabric bleeds, rinse it until the water runs clear. Do not use it in a quilt if it hasn't stopped bleeding. Hang the fabric to dry, or tumble it in the dryer until slightly damp; press well.

Select the Batting

For a small beginner project, a thin cotton batting is a good choice. It has a tendency to "stick" to fabric so it requires less basting. Also, it's easy to stitch. It's wise to follow the stitch density (distance between rows of stitching required to keep the batting from shifting and wadding up inside the quilt) recommendation printed on the packaging.

Polyester batting is lightweight and readily available. In general, it springs back to its original height when compressed, adding a puffiness to quilts. It tends to "beard" (work out between the weave of the fabric) more than natural fibers. Polyester fleece is denser and works well for pillow tops and place mats.

Wool batting has good loft retention and absorbs moisture, making it ideal for cool, damp climates. Read the label carefully before purchasing a wool batting because it may require special handling.

ROTARY CUTTING

We've taken the guesswork out of rotary cutting with this primer.

Plan for Cutting

Quilt-Lovers' Favorites™ instructions list pieces in the order in which they should be cut to make the best use of your fabrics. Always consider the fabric grain before cutting. The arrow on a pattern piece or template indicates which direction the fabric grain should run. One or more straight sides of the pattern piece or template should follow the fabric's lengthwise or crosswise grain.

The lengthwise grain, parallel to the selvage (the tightly finished edge), has the least amount of stretch. (Do not use the selvage of a woven fabric in a quilt. When washed, it may shrink more than the rest of the fabric.) Crosswise grain, perpendicular to the selvage, has a little more give. The edge of any pattern piece that will be on the outside of a block or quilt should always be cut on the lengthwise grain. Be sure to press the fabric before cutting to remove any wrinkles or folds.

Using a Rotary Cutter

When cutting, keep an even pressure on the rotary cutter and make sure the blade is touching the edge of the ruler.

continued

The less you move your fabric when cutting, the more accurate you'll be.

SQUARING UP THE FABRIC EDGE

Before rotary-cutting fabric into strips, it is imperative that one fabric edge be made straight, or squared up. Since all subsequent cuts will be measured from this straight edge, squaring up the fabric edge is an important step. There are several different techniques for squaring up an edge, some of which involve the use of a pair of rulers. For clarity and simplicity, we have chosen to describe a single-ruler technique here. *Note:* The instructions are for right-handers.

1. Lay your fabric on the rotary mat with the right side down and one selvage edge away from you. Fold the fabric with the wrong side inside and the selvages together. Fold the fabric in half again, lining up the fold with the selvage edges. Lightly hand-crease all of the folds.

2. Position the folded fabric on the cutting mat with the selvage edges away from you and the bulk of the fabric length to your left. With the ruler on top of the fabric, align a horizontal grid line on the ruler with the lower folded fabric edge, leaving about 1" of fabric exposed along the right-hand edge of the ruler (see Photo 1). Do not worry about or try to align the uneven raw edges along the right-hand side of the fabric. *Note:* If the grid lines on the cutting mat interfere with your ability to focus on the ruler grid lines, turn your cutting mat over and work on the unmarked side.

3. Hold the ruler firmly in place with your left hand, keeping your fingers away from the right-hand edge and spreading your fingers apart slightly. Apply pressure to the ruler with your fingertips to prevent it from slipping as you cut. With the ruler firmly in place, hold the rotary cutter so the blade is touching the right-hand edge of the ruler. Roll the blade along the ruler edge, beginning just off the folded edge and pushing the cutter away from you, toward the selvage edge.

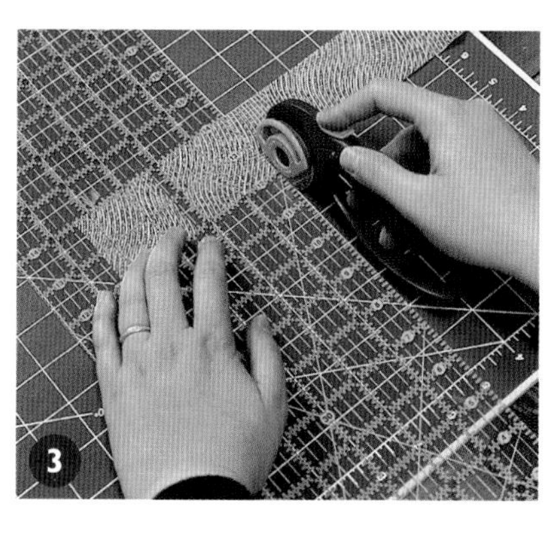

4. The fabric strip to the right of the ruler's edge should be cut cleanly away, leaving you with a straight edge from which you can measure all subsequent cuts. Do not pick up the fabric once the edge is squared; instead, turn the cutting mat to rotate the fabric and begin cutting strips.

CUTTING AND SUBCUTTING STRIPS

To use a rotary cutter to its greatest advantage, first cut a strip of fabric, then subcut the strip into specific sizes. For example, if your instructions say to cut forty 2" squares, follow these steps.

1. First cut a 2"-wide strip crosswise on the fabric. Assuming you have squared up the fabric edge as described earlier, you can turn your cutting mat clockwise 180° with the newly squared-up edge on your left and the excess fabric on the right. Place the ruler on top of the fabric.

2. Align the 2" grid mark on the ruler with the squared-up edge of the fabric (see Photo 2). *Note:* Align only the vertical grid mark and the fabric raw edge; ignore the selvages at the lower edge that may not line up perfectly with the horizontal ruler grid. A good rule of thumb to remember when rotary-cutting fabric is "the piece you want to keep should be under the ruler." That way, if you accidentally swerve away from the ruler when cutting, the piece under the ruler will be "safe."

3. Placing your rotary cutter along the ruler's right-hand edge and holding the ruler firmly with your left hand, run the blade along the ruler, as in Step 3 of Squaring Up the Fabric Edge, *left,* to cut the strip. Remove the ruler.

4. Sliding the excess fabric out of the way, carefully turn the mat so the 2" strip is horizontal in relation to you. Refer to Squaring Up the Fabric Edge to trim off the selvage edges and square up the strip's short edges.

5. Then align the ruler's 2" grid mark with a squared-up short edge of the strip (the 2" square you want to keep should be under the ruler). Hold the ruler with your left hand and run the rotary cutter along the right-hand ruler edge to cut a 2" square. You can cut multiple 2" squares from one strip by sliding the ruler over 2" from the previous cutting line and cutting again (see Photo 3). From a 44/45"-wide strip, you'll likely be able to cut twenty-one 2" squares. Since in this example you need a total of 40, cut a second 2"-wide strip and subcut it into 2" squares.

CUTTING TRIANGLES

Right triangles also can be quickly and accurately cut with a rotary cutter. There are two common ways to cut triangles. An example of each method follows.

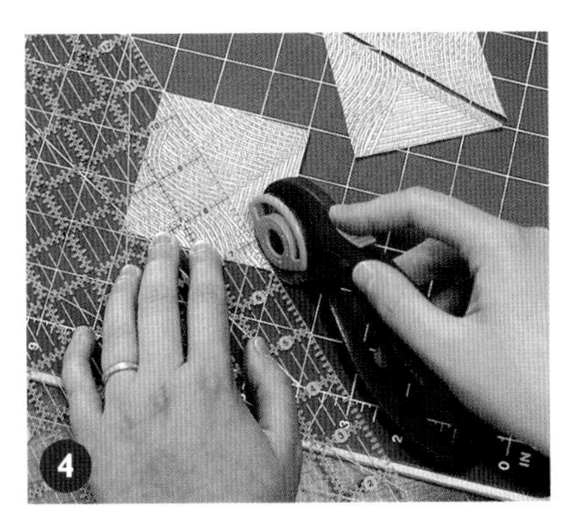

To cut two triangles from one square, the instructions may read:

From green print, cut:
- 20—3" squares, cutting each in half diagonally for a total of 40 triangles

1. Referring to Cutting and Subcutting Strips *opposite,* cut a 3"-wide fabric strip and subcut the strip into 3" squares.

2. Line up the ruler's edge with opposite corners of a square to cut it in half diagonally (see Photo 4). Cut along the ruler's edge. *Note:* The triangles' resultant long edges are on the bias. Avoid stretching or overhandling these edges when piecing so that seams don't become wavy and distorted.

To cut four triangles from one square, the instructions may read:

From green print, cut:
- 20—6" squares, cutting each diagonally twice in an X for a total of 80 triangles

3. Referring to Cutting and Subcutting Strips *opposite,* cut a 6"-wide fabric strip and subcut it into 6" squares.

4. Line up the ruler's edge with opposite corners of a square to cut it in half diagonally. Cut along the ruler's edge; do not separate the two triangles created. Line up the ruler's edge with the remaining corners and cut along the ruler's edge to make a total of four triangles (see Photo 5). *Note:* The triangles' resultant short edges are on the bias. Avoid stretching or overhandling these edges when piecing so that seams don't become wavy and distorted.

CUTTING WITH TEMPLATES

A successful quilt requires precise cutting of pieces.

About Scissors

Sharp scissor blades are vital to accurate cutting, but keeping them sharp is difficult because each use dulls the edges slightly. Cutting paper and plastic speeds the dulling process, so invest in a second pair for those materials and reserve your best scissors for fabric.

Make the Templates

For some quilts, you'll need to cut out the same shape multiple times. For accurate piecing later, the individual pieces should be identical to one another.

A template is a pattern made from extra-sturdy material so you can trace around it many times without wearing away the edges. You can make your own templates by duplicating printed patterns (like those on the Pattern Sheets) on plastic.

To make permanent templates, we recommend using easy-to-cut template plastic. This material lasts indefinitely, and its transparency allows you to trace the pattern directly onto its surface.

To make a template, lay the plastic over a printed pattern. Trace the pattern onto the plastic using a ruler and a permanent marker. This will ensure straight lines, accurate corners, and permanency. *Note:* If the pattern you are tracing is a half-pattern to begin with, you must first make a full-size pattern. To do so, fold a piece of tracing paper in half and crease; unfold. Lay the tracing paper over the half-pattern, aligning the crease with the fold line indicated on the pattern. Trace the half-pattern. Then rotate the tracing paper, aligning the half-pattern on the opposite side of the crease to trace the other half of the pattern. Use this full-size pattern to create your template.

For hand piecing and appliqué, make templates the exact size of the finished pieces, without seam allowances, by tracing the patterns' dashed lines. For machine piecing, make templates with the seam allowances included.

For easy reference, mark each template with its letter designation, grain line if noted, and block name. Verify the template's size by placing it over the printed pattern. Templates must be accurate or the error, however small, will compound many times as you assemble the quilt. To check the accuracy of your templates, make a test block before cutting the fabric pieces for an entire quilt.

continued

Trace the Templates

To mark on fabric, use a special quilt marker that makes a thin, accurate line. Do not use a ballpoint or ink pen that may bleed if washed. Test all marking tools on a fabric scrap before using them.

To trace pieces that will be used for hand piecing or appliqué, place templates facedown on the wrong side of the fabric; position the tracings at least ½" apart (see Diagram 1, template A). The lines drawn on the fabric are the sewing lines. Mark cutting lines, or estimate by eye a seam allowance around each piece as you cut out the pieces. For hand piecing, add a ¼" seam allowance when cutting out the pieces; for hand appliqué, add a 3⁄16" seam allowance.

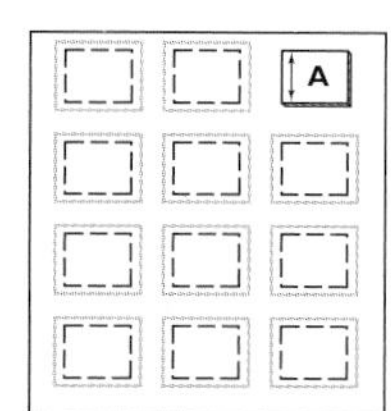

Diagram 1

Templates used to make pieces for machine piecing have seam allowances included so you can use common lines for efficient cutting. To trace, place templates facedown on the wrong side of the fabric; position them without space in between (see Diagram 2, template B). Using sharp scissors or a rotary cutter and ruler, cut precisely on the drawn (cutting) lines.

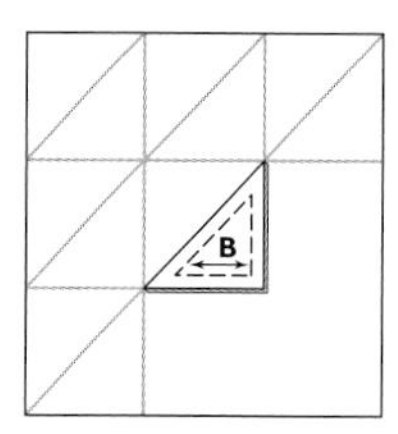

Diagram 2

Templates for Angled Pieces

When two patchwork pieces come together and form an angled opening, a third piece must be set into this angle. This happens frequently when using diamond shapes.

For a design that requires setting in, a pinhole or window template makes it easy to mark the fabric with each shape's exact sewing and cutting lines and the exact point of each corner on the sewing line. By matching the corners of adjacent pieces, you'll be able to sew them together easily and accurately.

To make a pinhole template, lay template plastic over a pattern piece. Trace both the cutting and sewing lines onto the plastic. Carefully cut out the template on the cutting line. Using a sewing-machine needle or any large needle, make a hole in the template at each corner on the sewing line (matching points). The holes must be large enough for a pencil point or other fabric marker to poke through.

Trace Angled Pieces

To mark fabric using a pinhole template, lay it facedown on the wrong side of the fabric and trace. Using a pencil, mark dots on the fabric through the holes in the template to create matching points, then cut out the fabric piece on the drawn line.

To mark fabric using a window template, lay it facedown on the wrong side of the fabric (see Diagram 3). With a marking tool, mark the cutting line, sewing line, and each corner on the sewing line (matching points). Cut out the fabric piece on the cutting lines, making sure all pieces have sewing lines and matching points marked.

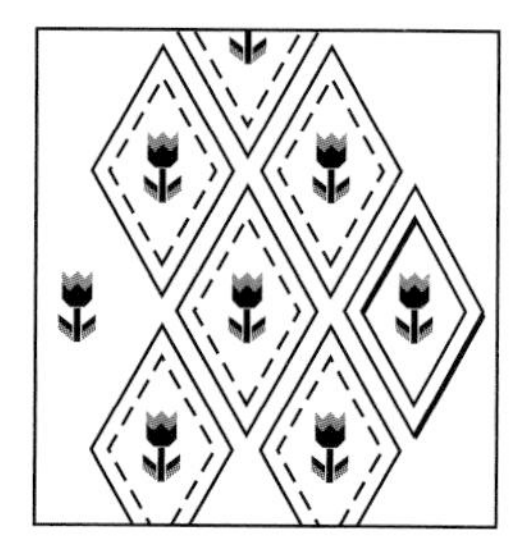

Diagram 3

Piecing

Patchwork piecing consists of sewing fabric pieces together in a specific pattern.

Hand Piecing

In hand piecing, seams are sewn only on the marked sewing lines; the seam allowances remain unstitched. Begin by matching the edges of two pieces with the fabrics' right sides together. Sewing lines should be marked on the wrong side of both pieces. Push a pin through both fabric layers at each corner (see Diagram 1). Secure the pins perpendicular to the sewing line. Insert more pins between the corners.

Insert a needle through both fabrics at the seam-line corner. Make one or two backstitches atop the first stitch to secure the thread. Weave the needle in and out of the fabric along the seam line, taking four to six tiny stitches at a time before you pull the thread taut (see Diagram 2). Remove the pins as you sew. Turn the work over occasionally to see that the stitching follows the marked sewing line on the other side.

Sew eight to 10 stitches per inch along the seam line. At the end of the seam, remove the last pin and make the ending stitch through the hole left

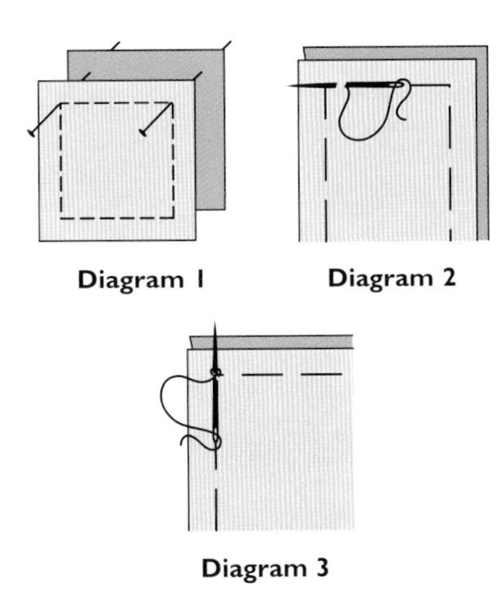
Diagram 1 Diagram 2

Diagram 3

by the corner pin. Backstitch over the last stitch and end the seam with a loop knot (see Diagram 3).

To join rows of patchwork by hand, hold the sewn pieces with right sides together and seams matched. Insert pins at the corners of the matching pieces. Add additional pins as necessary, securing each pin perpendicular to the sewing line (see Diagram 4).

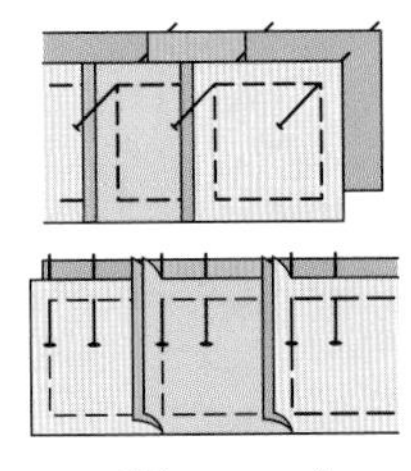
Diagram 4

Stitch the joining seam as before, but do not sew across the seam allowances that join the patches. At each seam allowance, make a backstitch or loop knot, then slide the needle through the seam allowance (see Diagram 5). Knot or backstitch again to give the intersection strength, then sew the remainder of the seam. Press each seam as it is completed.

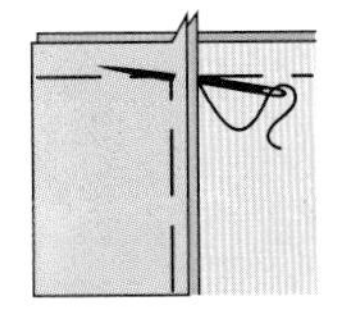
Diagram 5

Machine Piecing

Machine piecing depends on sewing an exact ¼" seam allowance. Some machines have a presser foot that is the proper width, or a ¼" foot is available. To check the width of a machine's presser foot, sew a sample seam with the raw fabric edges aligned with the right edge of the presser foot; measure the resultant seam allowance using graph paper with a ¼" grid.

Using two different thread colors—one on top of the machine and one in the bobbin—can help you to better match your thread color to your fabrics. If your quilt has many fabrics, use a neutral color, such as gray or beige, for both the top and bobbin threads throughout the quilt.

Press for Success

In quilting, almost every seam needs to be pressed before the piece is sewn to another, so keep your iron and ironing board near your sewing area. It's important to remember to press with an up and down motion. Moving the iron around on the fabric can distort seams, especially those sewn on the bias.

Project instructions in this book generally tell you in what direction to press each seam. When in doubt, press both seam allowances toward the darker fabric. When joining rows of blocks, alternate the direction the seam allowances are pressed to ensure flat corners.

Setting in Pieces

The key to sewing angled pieces together is aligning marked matching points carefully. Whether you're stitching by machine or hand, start and stop sewing precisely at the matching points (see the dots in Diagram 6, top) and backstitch to secure the ends of the seams. This prepares the angle for the next piece to be set in.

Join two diamond pieces, sewing between matching points to make an angled unit (see Diagram 6).

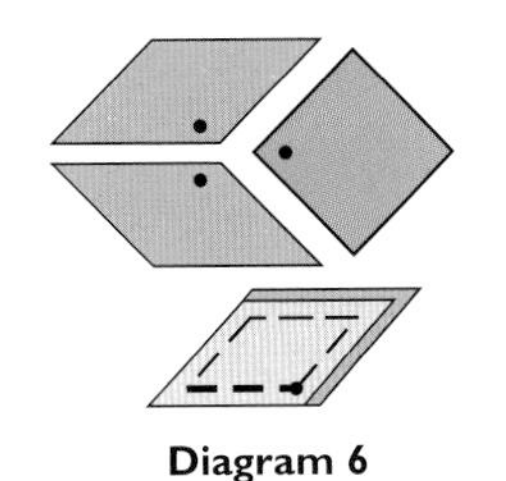
Diagram 6

Follow the specific instructions for either machine or hand piecing to complete the set-in seam.

MACHINE PIECING

With right sides together, pin one piece of the angled unit to one edge of the square (see Diagram 7). Match the seam's matching points by pushing a pin through both fabric layers to check the alignment. Machine-stitch the seam between the matching points. Backstitch to secure the ends of the seam; do not stitch into the ¼" seam allowance. Remove the unit from the sewing machine.

Bring the adjacent edge of the angled unit up and align it with the next edge of the square (see Diagram 8). Insert a pin in each corner to align matching points, then pin the remainder of the seam. Machine-stitch between matching points as before. Press the seam allowances of the set-in piece away from it.

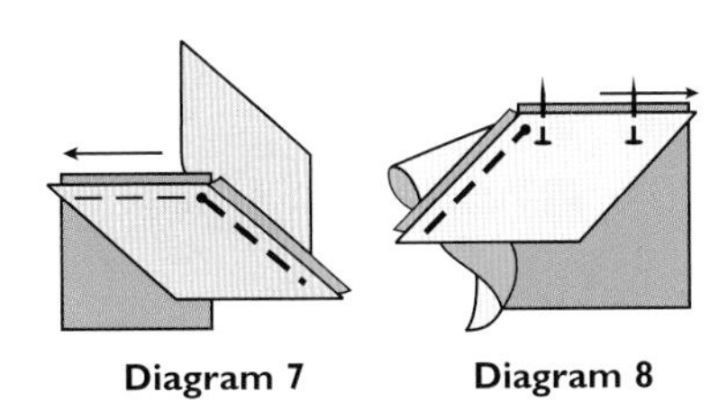
Diagram 7 Diagram 8

HAND PIECING

Pin one piece of the angled unit to one edge of the square with right sides together (see Diagram 9). Use pins to align matching points at the corners.

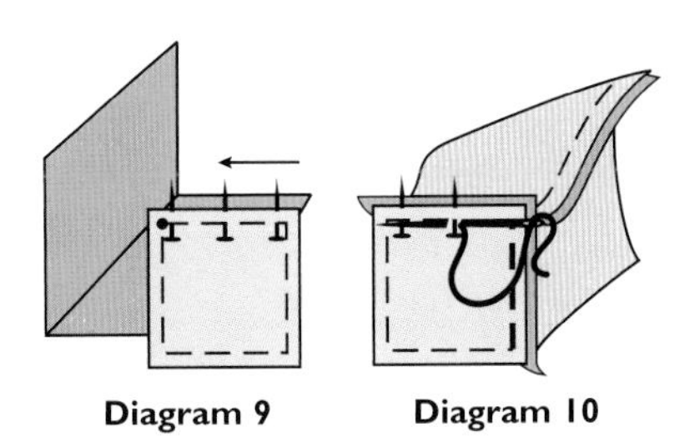
Diagram 9 Diagram 10

Hand-sew the seam from the open end of the angle into the corner. Remove pins as you sew between matching points. Backstitch at the corner to secure stitches. Do not sew into the ¼" seam allowance and do not cut your thread.

continued

Bring the adjacent edge of the square up and align it with the other edge of the angled unit. Insert a pin in each corner to align matching points, then pin the remainder of the seam (see Diagram 10 on *page 155*). Continuing the thread from the previous seam, hand-sew the seam from the corner to the open end of the angle, removing pins as you sew. Press the seam allowances of the set-in piece away from it.

Mitered Border Corners

A border surrounds the piecework of many quilts. Angled, mitered corners add to a border's framed effect.

To add a border with mitered corners, first pin a border strip to a quilt top edge, matching the center of the strip and the center of the quilt top edge. Allow excess border fabric to extend beyond the edges. Sew together, beginning and ending the seam ¼" from the quilt top corners (see Diagram 11). Repeat with the remaining border strips. Press the seam allowances toward the border strips.

Overlap the border strips at each corner (see Diagram 12). Align the edge of a 90° right triangle with the raw edge of a top border strip so the long edge of the triangle intersects the seam in the corner. With a pencil, draw along the edge of the triangle from the border seam out to the raw edge. Place the bottom border strip on top and repeat the marking process.

With the right sides of adjacent border strips together, match the marked seam lines and pin (see Diagram 13).

Beginning with a backstitch at the inside corner, stitch exactly on the marked lines to the outside edges of the border strips. Check the right side of the corner to see that it lies flat. Then trim the excess fabric, leaving a ¼" seam allowance. Press the seam open. Mark and sew the remaining corners in the same manner.

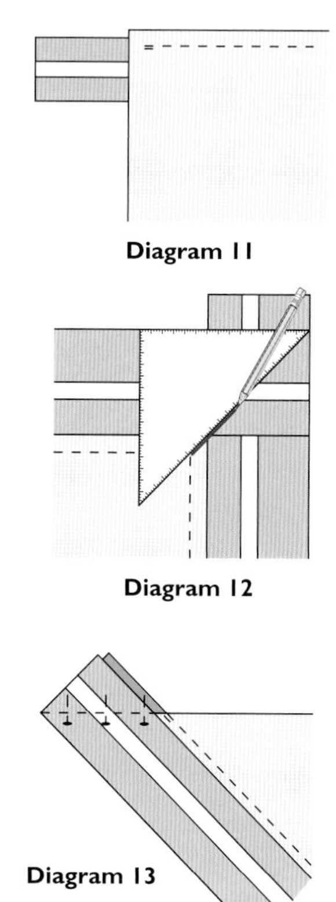
Diagram 11

Diagram 12

Diagram 13

APPLIQUÉ

With appliqué, you create a picture by stitching fabric shapes atop a fabric foundation.

Start Simple

We encourage beginners to select an appliqué design with straight lines and gentle curves. Learning to make sharp points and tiny stitches takes practice.

In the following instructions, we've used a stemmed flower motif as the appliqué example.

Baste the Seam Allowances

Begin by turning under the 3⁄16" seam allowances on the appliqué pieces; press. Some quilters like to thread-baste the folded edges to ensure proper placement. Edges that will be covered by other pieces don't need to be turned under.

For sharp points on tips, first trim the seam allowance to within ⅛" of the stitching line (see Photo 1, *opposite*), tapering the sides gradually to 3⁄16". Fold under the seam allowance remaining on the tips. Then turn the seam allowances under on both sides of the tips. The side seam allowances will overlap slightly at the tips, forming sharp points.

Baste the folded edges in place (see Photo 2, *opposite*). The turned seam allowances may form little pleats on the back side that you also should baste in place. Remove the basting stitches after the shapes have been appliquéd to the foundation.

Make Bias Stems

In order to curve gracefully, appliqué stems are cut on the bias. The strips for stems can be prepared in two ways. You can fold and press the strip in thirds as shown in Photo 3, *opposite*. Or you can fold the bias strip in half lengthwise with the wrong side inside; press. Stitch ¼" in from the raw edges to keep them aligned. Fold the strip in half again, hiding the raw edges behind the first folded edge; press.

Position and Stitch

Pin the prepared appliqué pieces in place on the foundation (see Photo 4, *opposite*) using the position markings or referring to the block assembly diagram. If your pattern suggests it, mark the position for each piece on the foundation before you begin. Overlap the flowers and stems as indicated.

Using thread in colors that match the fabrics, sew each stem and blossom onto the foundation with small slip stitches as shown in Photo 5. (For photographic purposes, thread color does not match fabric color.)

Catch only a few threads of the stem or flower fold with each stitch. Pull the stitches taut, but not so tight that they pucker the fabric. You can use the needle's point to manipulate the appliqué edges as needed. Take an extra slip stitch at the point of a petal to secure it to the foundation.

You can use hand-quilting needles for appliqué stitching, but some quilters prefer a longer milliner's or straw needle. The extra needle length aids in tucking fabric under before taking slip stitches.

If the foundation fabric shows through the appliqué fabrics, cut away the foundation fabric. Trimming the foundation fabric also reduces the bulk of multiple layers when quilting later. Carefully trim the underlying fabric to within ¼" of the appliqué stitches (see Photo 6) and avoid cutting the appliqué fabrics.

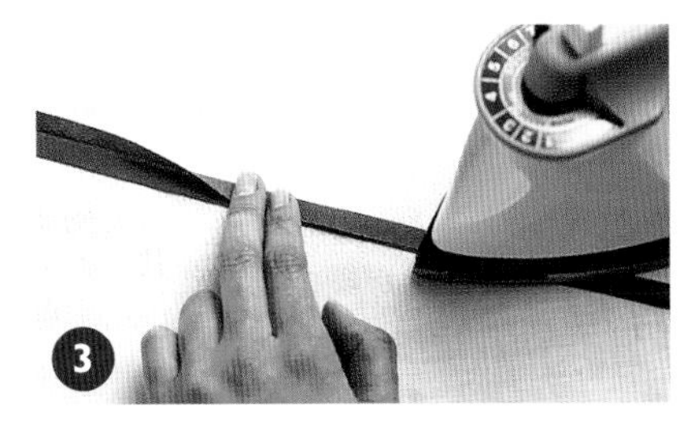

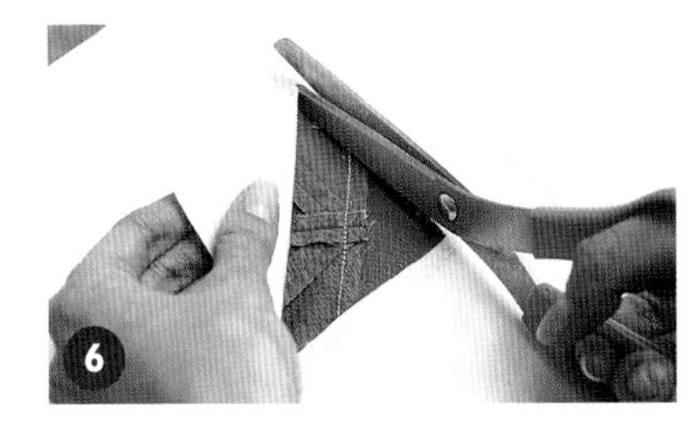

Fusible Appliqué

For quick-finish appliqué, use paper-backed lightweight fusible web. Then you can iron the shapes onto the foundation and add decorative stitching to the edges. This product consists of two layers, a fusible webbing lightly bonded to paper that peels off. The webbing adds a slight stiffness to the back of the appliqué pieces.

When you purchase this product, read the directions on the bolt end or packaging to make sure you're buying the right kind for your project. Some brands are specifically engineered to bond fabrics with no sewing at all. If you try to stitch fabric after it has bonded with one of these products, you may encounter difficulty. Some paper-backed fusible products are made exclusively for sewn edges; others work with or without stitching.

If you buy paper-backed fusible web from a bolt, be sure fusing instructions are included because the iron temperature and timing varies by brand. This information is usually on the paper backing.

With any of these products, the general procedure is to trace the patterns wrong side up onto the paper side of the fusible web. Then place the fusible-web pieces on the wrong side of the appliqué fabrics, paper side up, and use an iron to fuse the layers together. Then cut out the fabric shapes, peel off the paper, turn the fabrics right side up, and fuse them to the foundation fabric.

You also can fuse the fusible web and fabric together before tracing. You'll still need to trace templates wrong side up on the paper backing.

If you've used a no-sew fusible web, your appliqué is done. If not, finish the edges with hand or machine stitching.

Cutting Bias Strips

Strips for curved appliqué pattern pieces, such as meandering vines, and for binding curved edges should be cut on the bias, which runs at a 45° angle to the selvage of a woven fabric and has the most give or stretch.

To cut bias strips, begin with a fabric square or rectangle. Use a large acrylic ruler to square up the left edge of the fabric. Then make a cut at a 45° angle to the left edge (see Bias Strip Diagram). Handle the diagonal edges carefully to avoid distorting the bias. To cut a strip, measure the desired width parallel to the 45° cut edge; cut. Continue cutting enough strips to total the length needed.

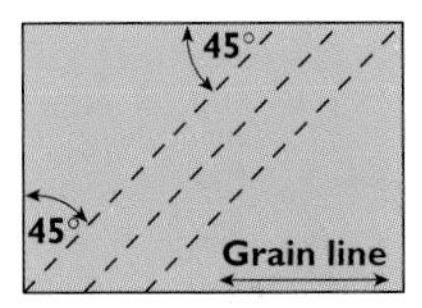

Bias Strip Diagram

Covered Cording

Finish pillows and quilts with easy, tailored cording.

Covered cording is made by sewing a bias-cut fabric strip around a length of cording. The width of the bias strip varies according to the diameter of your cording. Refer to the specific project instructions for those measurements. Regardless, the method used to cover the cording is the same.

With the wrong side inside, fold under 1½" at one end of the bias strip. With the wrong side inside, fold the strip in half lengthwise to make the cording cover. Insert the cording next to the folded edge, placing a cording end 1" from the cording cover folded end. Using a machine cording foot, sew through both fabric layers right next to the cording (see Diagram 1).

When attaching the cording to your project, begin stitching 1½" from the covered cording's folded end. Round the corners slightly, making sure the corner curves match. As you stitch each corner, gently ease the covered cording into place (see Diagram 2).

After going around the entire edge of the project, cut the end of the cording so that it will fit snugly into the folded opening at the beginning (see Diagram 3). The ends of the cording should abut inside the covering. Stitch the ends in place to secure (see Diagram 4).

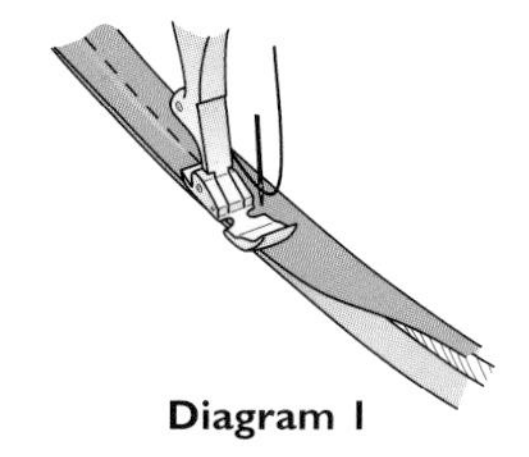

Diagram 1

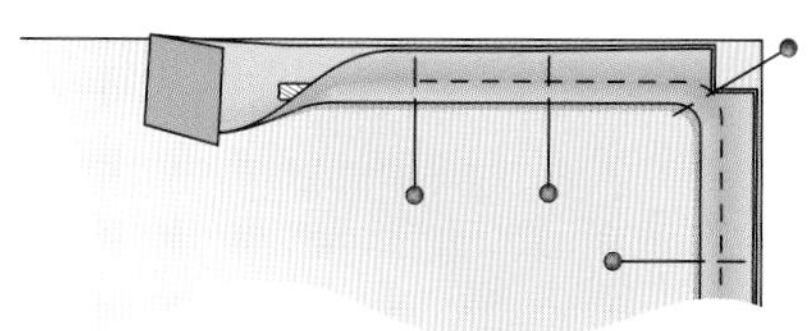

Diagram 2

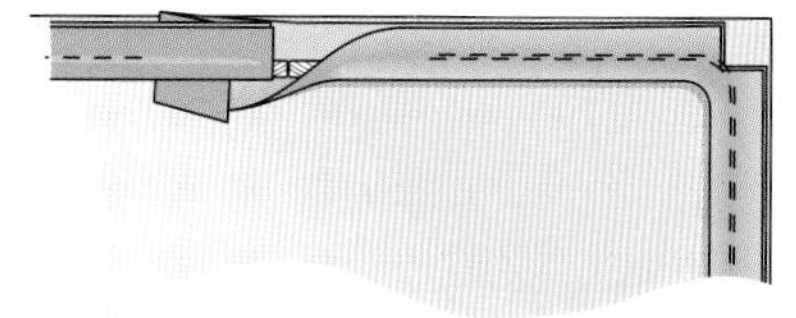

Diagram 3

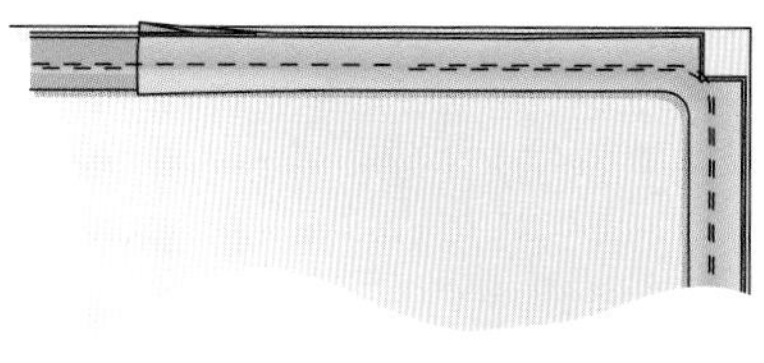

Diagram 4

Hanging Sleeves

When you want a favorite quilt to become wall art, hang it with care to avoid sagging, tearing, and wavy edges.

Quilts make wonderful pieces of wall art. When treated as museum pieces and hung properly, they won't deteriorate. Let size be your guide when determining how to hang your quilt.

Hang smaller quilts, a 25" square or less, with purchased clips, sewn-on tabs, or pins applied to the corners. Larger quilts require a hanging sleeve attached to the back. It may take a few minutes more to sew on a sleeve, but the effort preserves your hours of work with less distortion and damage.

Make a Hanging Sleeve

1. Measure the quilt's top edge.

2. Cut a 6"- to 10"-wide strip of prewashed fabric 2" longer than the quilt's top edge. For example, if the top edge is 40", cut a 6×42" strip. A 6"-wide strip is sufficient for a dowel or drapery rod. If you're using something bigger in diameter, cut a wider fabric strip. If you're sending your quilt to be displayed at a quilt show, adjust your

Diagram 1

Diagram 2

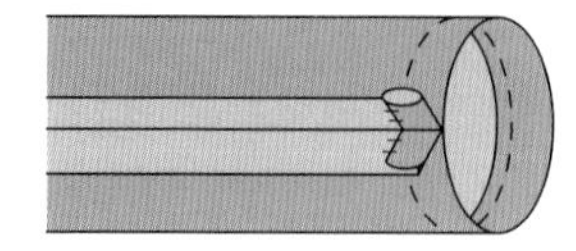

Diagram 3

measurements to accommodate the show's requirements.

3. Fold under 1½" on both ends of the fabric strip. Sew ¼" from the raw edges (see Diagram 1).

4. Fold the fabric strip in half lengthwise with the wrong side inside; pin. Stitch together the long edges with a ¼" seam allowance (see Diagram 2) to make the sleeve. Press the seam allowance open and center the seam in the middle of the sleeve (see Diagram 3).

5. Center the sleeve on the quilt back about 1" below the binding with the seam facing the back (see Diagram 4). Slip-stitch the sleeve to the quilt along both long edges and the portions of the short edges that touch the back, stitching through the back and batting.

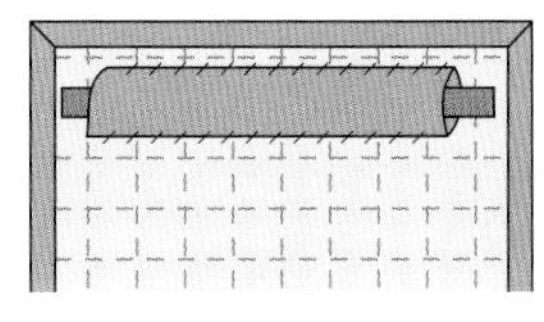
Diagram 4

6. Slide a wooden dowel or slender piece of wood that is 1" longer than the finished sleeve into the sleeve and hang as desired.

FINISHING

The final step in quiltmaking is to bind the edges.

Layering

Cut and piece the backing fabric to measure at least 3" bigger on all sides than the quilt top. Press all seam allowances open. With wrong sides together, layer the quilt top and backing fabric with the batting in between; baste. Quilt as desired.

Binding

The binding for most quilts is cut on the straight grain of the fabric. If your quilt has curved edges, cut the strips on the bias (see *page 157*). The cutting instructions for projects in this book specify the number of binding strips or a total length needed to finish the quilt. The instructions also specify enough width for a French-fold, or double-layer, binding because it's easier to apply and adds durability.

Join the strips with diagonal seams to make one continuous binding strip (see Diagram 1). Trim the excess fabric, leaving ¼" seam allowances. Press the seam allowances open. Then, with the wrong sides together, fold under 1" at one end of the binding strip (see Diagram 2); press. Fold the strip in half lengthwise (see Diagram 3); press.

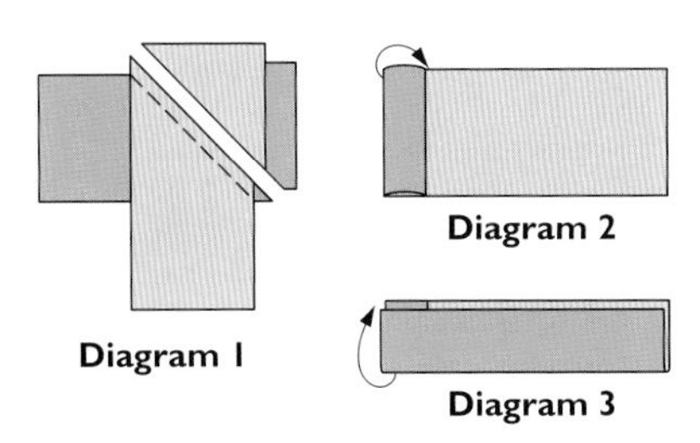
Diagram 1

Diagram 2

Diagram 3

Beginning in the center of one side, place the binding strip against the right side of the quilt top, aligning the binding strip's raw edges with the quilt top's raw edge (see Diagram 4). Beginning 1½" from the folded edge, sew through all layers, stopping ¼" from the corner. Backstitch, then clip the threads. Remove the quilt from under the sewing-machine presser foot.

Fold the binding strip upward (see Diagram 5), creating a diagonal fold, and finger-press.

Holding the diagonal fold in place with your finger, bring the binding strip down in line with the next edge, making a horizontal fold that aligns with the first edge of the quilt (see Diagram 6).

Start sewing again at the top of the horizontal fold, stitching through all layers. Sew around the quilt, turning each corner in the same manner.

When you return to the starting point, lap the binding strip inside the beginning fold (see Diagram 7).

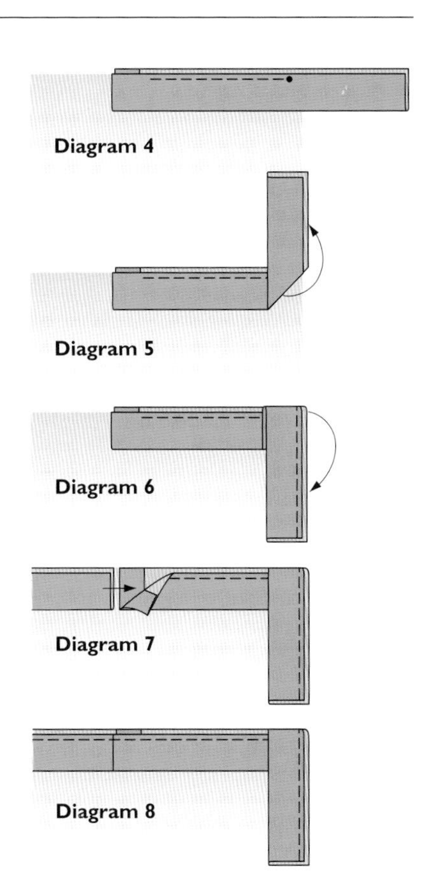
Diagram 4

Diagram 5

Diagram 6

Diagram 7

Diagram 8

Finish sewing to the starting point (see Diagram 8). Trim the batting and backing fabric even with the quilt top edges.

Turn the binding over the edge of the quilt to the back. Hand-stitch the binding to the backing fabric, making sure to cover any machine stitching.

To make mitered corners on the back, hand-stitch the binding up to a corner; fold a miter in the binding. Take a stitch or two in the fold to secure it. Then stitch the binding in place up to the next corner. Finish each corner in the same manner.

CREDITS

Quilt Designers

Betty Alvarez
Bali Ho
Designer Betty Alvarez of Marietta, Georgia, a quilter since 1978, enjoys quilts that showcase a variety of fabrics.

Janey Edwards and Roxie Wood
Sweet Cherries
Roxie Wood, owner of Thimble Creek Quilts in Walnut Creek, California, and Janey Edwards, the shop's former co-owner, collaborated on this project to highlight a favorite fabric. They say it's easier to select companion fabrics when your main fabric has many colors in it.

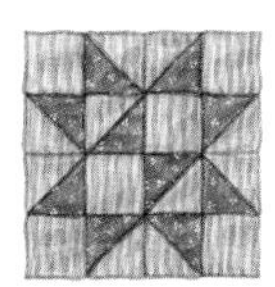

Andria and Sarah Grant
Flickering Stars
Andria Grant and her mother, Sarah Grant, joined forces to piece this lap-size quilt. Andria enjoys teaching beginning quilters, and this project is perfect for fine-tuning rotary-cutting skills.

Mary Jo Hiney
Rule the Roost
Pattern designer Mary Jo Hiney of Los Osos, California, is prolific when it comes to producing foundation-pieced quilts. She even has written books on this precise technique.

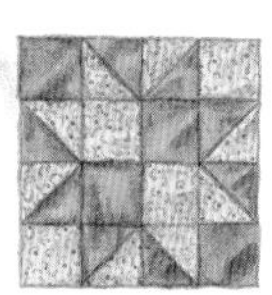

Joy Hoffman
Sunrise, Sunset
Joy Hoffman of Redwood Falls, Minnesota, started quilting in her teens. She likes making traditional blocks using new fabric combinations and techniques.

Judy Martin
Centennial Pineapple
In her 35 years of making quilts, designer Judy Martin of Grinnell, Iowa, has perfected her rotary-cutting and piecing skills. To date, she has published more than 15 books.

Mabeth Oxenreider
Sunshine and Shade
Teacher and award-winning quilter Mabeth Oxenreider of Carlisle, Iowa, has worked full-time in the quilting business since 1980. She teaches across the country and uses multiple techniques—from foundation-piecing to machine-trapunto—to complete projects in a range of sizes—from miniature to bed-size.

Karen Stone
Mississippi Wheel of Fortune
Designer and author Karen Stone of Dallas, Texas, specializes in foundation piecing and uses it to produce complex blocks. Karen's confidence with color makes each of her quilts a lesson in fabric selection.

Mary Ellen Von Holt
Jacob's Ladder
Mary Ellen Von Holt started quilting more than 25 years ago. For the past 20 years, she has partnered with quilters Alice Berg and Sylvia Johnson. The trio designs patterns and booklets, writes books, and operates a quilt shop, Little Quilts, in Marietta, Georgia.

Tonee White
Twelve Trumpets
Quiltmaker Tonee White of Scottsdale, Arizona, combines appliquéing and quilting into one step when she teaches her "appliquilt" technique. Tonee says the result is a folk-art look in less time than when you use traditional methods.

Laura Boehnke
Quilt Tester
With a keen color sense and astute use of fabrics, quilt tester Laura Boehnke gives each project an entirely different look when she verifies a pattern, a job she's been doing for *American Patchwork & Quilting*® magazine since its inception.

Project Quilters and Finishers

Laura Boehnke
Maryless Elden
Karen Gilson, Walnut Creek Quilting
Becky Goldsmith
Kate Hardy
Roseann Kermes
Jill Abeloe Mead
Cindy Taylor Oates
Mabeth Oxenreider
Julie Pralle
Shelly Robson
Janelle Swenson
Sue Urich
April West
Molly Zearing

Materials Suppliers

Benartex
Chanteclaire
Hoffman Fabrics
Moda
Northcott Silk
P&B Textiles
Red Rooster Fabrics
RJR Fabrics
Robert Kaufman Fine Fabrics
Springs
Timeless Treasures

Photographers

Craig Anderson: pages 13, 41, 52, 54, 55, 57, 63, 77, 83, 101, 102, 135
Marcia Cameron: pages 38, 39, 53, 61, 72, 80, 107, 114, 125, 134
Bill Hopkins: pages 96, 124
Scott Little: pages 21, 30, 44, 65, 85, 104, 126, 129, 149
Andy Lyons: pages 14, 29, 31, 81, 92, 128
Peter Krumhardt: pages 74, 138, 147
Blaine Moats: pages 12, 23, 33, 46, 75, 82, 103, 111, 118, 136, 139
Greg Scheidemann: pages 19, 43, 108, 127
Perry Struse: pages 8, 16, 22, 25, 37, 38, 43, 47, 48, 59, 62, 69, 86, 91, 98, 100, 110, 112, 117, 119, 123, 131, 141, 146
Steve Struse: pages 10, 27, 60, 70, 79, 89, 106, 133, 144, 145